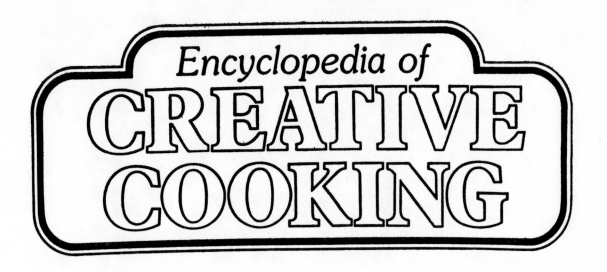

Encyclopedia of CREATIVE COOKING

Volume 11
Desserts

D1303144

Editors for U.S. editions
Steve Sherman and Julia Older

ECB Enterprises Inc.

All about Batters, Custards and Rice Desserts

Individual Crème Caramels

Crêpes

It has been the custom to leave crêpe batter to stand for a while before cooking, but experiments have shown that this makes no difference to the final results. Cooked crêpes will keep for a week if wrapped in foil and stored in the refrigerator. Reheat the crêpes in a lightly greased hot pan, turning once.

Basic Crêpes

1 cup + 2 tablespoons flour
½ teaspoon salt
1 egg
1¼ cups milk
oil for frying

1 Sift the flour and salt into a bowl. Add the egg and half of the milk and beat thoroughly until smooth. Mix in the remaining milk and beat until bubbly.

2 Put the oil for frying in a heat-

Basic Crêpes, cooked to perfection and served with spoonfuls of your favorite jam, are a warming breakfast dish

---

proof pitcher. Pour a little of the oil into a 6-inch skillet over a fairly high heat. Tilt the pan to coat with oil, then pour any excess back into the pitcher.

3 When the pan is hot, pour in a little batter, tilting the pan to thinly coat the base. Cook quickly, shaking the pan and loosening the edge with a spatula, until the underside is golden brown. Toss the crêpe and cook the second side.

4 Slide the cooked crêpe out onto a plate and keep it warm, covered with a second plate. Repeat with the remaining batter, to make 8-10 crêpes.

5 Fold the crêpes into quarters and serve with jam.

Serves 4

Brandy and Orange Crêpes

Basic Crêpe batter
finely grated rind 1 orange
¼ cup sugar
¼ cup butter
juice 2 oranges
6 tablespoons brandy

1 Make up the batter, adding the grated orange rind with the egg, and make the crêpes following the instructions for the Basic Crêpe recipe. Fold the crêpes in quarters.

2 Gently heat the sugar in a skillet, shaking the pan, until the sugar is golden brown. Remove the pan from the heat and add the butter, orange juice and half of the brandy.

3 Place the folded crêpes in the pan and simmer for a few minutes, spooning on the sauce.

4 Warm the remaining brandy, pour it over the crêpes, ignite and serve immediately.

Serves 4

Brandy and Orange Crêpes are a variation of the famous Crêpes Suzette. You can prepare this dish well in advance

Pear Crêpe Cake

1½ recipes Basic Crêpe batter
2 tablespoons butter
¼ cup flour
1¼ cups milk
2 pears, peeled, quartered and
    cored
2 tablespoons pistachios
2 tablespoons sugar
few drops almond extract
⅓ cup apricot jam

1 Make the crêpes following the instructions for the basic recipe (see page 962). Pile the crêpes flat and keep them warm between two plates while making the sauce.

2 Preheat the oven to 375°F. Melt the butter in a pan, stir in the flour and cook over low heat for 2 minutes. Gradually stir in the milk, bring to a boil and simmer for 3 minutes, stirring continuously.

3 Slice the pears thinly. Skin and chop the pistachios. Add the pears and pistachios to the sauce with the sugar and almond extract and warm through.

4 Place a crêpe on a serving dish and spread it evenly with 2 teaspoons of the jam and some of the sauce. Place another crêpe on top and spread with jam and sauce. Continue to layer crêpes in the same way, finishing with a plain crêpe.

5 Place the crêpe cake in the oven for 10 minutes to heat through. Serve hot, cut into wedges.

Serves 8

Lemon Surprise Crêpes

⅔ cup sour cream
2 tablespoons sugar
finely grated rind and juice 1
    lemon
Basic Crêpe batter

Pear Crêpe Cake — wafer-thin crêpes layered with sweet apricot jam and a delicious pear and pistachio sauce

1 teaspoon ground ginger
8-10 scoops vanilla ice cream

1 Make the lemon sauce by mixing together the sour cream, sugar, lemon rind and juice.

2 Make up the crêpe batter, adding the ginger with the flour. Make the crêpes following the instructions for the Basic Crêpe recipe (see page 962). Pile the crêpes flat and keep them warm between two plates.

3 When all the crêpes are cooked, put a scoop of ice cream onto each and fold the crêpe in half. Serve immediately with the lemon sauce.

Serves 4

Apple-Pear Crêpes

Basic Crêpe batter
1 teaspoon cinnamon
2 red apples

Chocolate Walnut Crêpes

Basic Crêpe batter
⅓ cup raisins
3 tablespoons rum
¼ cup butter
1 cup very finely chopped walnuts
¾ cup sugar
½ teaspoon vanilla extract
3 tablespoons light cream

For the Chocolate Sauce:
4 ozs. milk chocolate
2 teaspoons cornstarch
1 cup milk
2 teaspoons sugar
3 tablespoons light cream
½ teaspoon cinnamon

1 First make the walnut filling: soak the raisins in the rum for 15 minutes. Soften the butter and blend in the walnuts, sugar, vanilla and cream. Mix well, then add the rum and fruit.

2 Make the chocolate sauce: break the chocolate into a small pan and add 3 tablespoons cold water. Stir over gentle heat until melted and smooth. Blend the cornstarch with a little of the milk and stir into the chocolate with the sugar and remaining milk. Gradually bring to a boil and simmer for 5 minutes, stirring. Remove from the heat and stir in the cream and cinnamon.

3 Make the crêpes following the instructions for the Basic Crêpe recipe (see page 962). Put a little of the walnut filling onto each cooked crêpe, roll up the crêpes and transfer to a heated serving dish. Cover and keep warm.

4 Gently reheat the chocolate sauce and pour it over the crêpes. Serve immediately.

Serves 4

3 pears
¼ cup sugar
1 tablespoon cornstarch
juice 1 orange
3 tablespoons apricot jam
sugar for sprinkling

1 Make up the batter, adding the cinnamon with the flour. Make the crêpes following the instructions for the Basic Crêpe recipe (see page 962). Pile the crêpes flat and keep them warm between two plates while making the filling.

2 Quarter the apples and pears, remove the cores and cut the fruit into chunks.

3 Place the sugar in a pan with 1¼

Apple-Pear Crêpes are easy to prepare and are sure to become a favorite with your family for winter suppers

cups cold water and stir over low heat until dissolved. Blend the cornstarch with the orange juice and stir into the pan with apricot jam. Bring to a boil and simmer for 3 minutes, stirring continuously.

4 Put some of the filling in the middle of each crêpe, roll up the crêpes and transfer to a heated serving dish. Sprinkle with a little sugar and serve.

Serves 4

965

Fritters

Fritters are among the most versatile of dishes, and you can dip and deep-fry almost anything. Use a basic crêpe recipe (see page 962), but halve the quantity of milk to make a thicker batter.

Fritters are lighter and crisper if the batter is very smooth. The oil used for deep frying should be just the right temperature: test it by dropping in a little batter. The drop should rise at once to the surface, but only brown after 2 or 3 minutes.

Cinnamon Apple Rings

4 apples
juice 1 lemon
1 teaspoon cinnamon
1¼ cups batter
oil for deep frying

1 Core and peel the apples, cut in horizontal slices, and sprinkle them with lemon juice.

2 Mix the cinnamon well into the batter. Heat the oil to 375°F. Dip the apple rings into the batter and deep-fry until crisp and golden. Drain and serve sprinkled with sugar.

Serves 4

Cinnamon Apple Rings — all the great natural flavor of fresh apples enclosed in a crisp cinnamon-flavored batter

Cherry Fritters

⅔ cups water
½ tablespoon sugar
¼ cup butter
1 cup all-purpose flour
pinch salt
3 eggs, beaten
oil for deep frying

For the Sauce:
1 lb. tart cherries
2½ cups water
¾ cup sugar
1 tablespoon cornstarch
1 teaspoon cherry-flavored liqueur (optional)

1 Place the water, sugar and butter in a large pan and bring them to a boil. Remove the pan from the heat.

2 Stir in the sifted flour and the salt and mix thoroughly. Place the pan back on the heat and stir the mixture continuously until it leaves the sides of the pan. Allow it to cool.

3 Add the beaten eggs to the paste, little by little, beating all the time until the paste is thick and of a dropping consistency.

4 Heat the oil in a deep fryer to 375°F. Take tablespoonfuls of the paste and drop them into the oil. Fry until they are crisp and golden brown. Remove with a slotted spoon and drain on absorbent paper. Keep warm.

5 To make the sauce, boil the cherries, water and sugar in a pan for 5 minutes. Strain the cherries from the syrup and boil the syrup until thickened, stirring in the cornstarch, which has been dissolved in a little water, to thicken further. Flavor if wished with liqueur. Split each fritter, top with a few cherries and serve with the cherry syrup.

Serves 6–8

Cherry Fritters are a crisp and sugary treat which can be served with a delicious cherry-flavored sauce

Look 'n Cook German Doughnuts

1 The ingredients **2** Mix the flour, sugar and salt, and sift three-quarters of the mixture into a bowl **3** Blend the yeast with lukewarm milk **4** Make a well in the sifted flour mixture and pour in the yeast and milk. Add the remaining flour mixture **5** Add the beaten eggs and oil, and mix well **6** Knead the dough until it is smooth **7** Place the dough in a floured bowl, cover with a damp cloth and let rise in a warm place. The risen

dough should spring back when pressed lightly with the fingertip **8** Turn the dough onto a floured surface and knead in the rum **9** Cut the dough into 12 equal-sized pieces **10** Roll each piece into a ball and let rise **11** Fry the doughnuts in deep hot oil, drain and roll in sugar **12** Make an incision in each doughnut with a knife and insert the jam

German Doughnuts

3½ cups flour
¼ cup sugar
1 teaspoon salt
¾ cup milk
1 tablespoon yeast
2 tablespoons oil
2 eggs
2 teaspoons rum
oil for deep frying
sugar for coating
6 tablespoons red jam

1 Mix the flour, sugar and salt, and sift three-quarters of the mixture into a large bowl.

2 Heat the milk to lukewarm and blend gradually into the yeast. Make a well in the center of the sifted flour mixture and pour in the yeast and milk. Sift the remaining flour mixture into the bowl.

3 Beat together oil and eggs and add to the bowl. Mix well with a wooden spoon, then turn onto a lightly floured surface and knead to a soft, smooth dough.

4 Place the dough in a clean, floured bowl, cover with a damp cloth and let rise in a warm place for 45 minutes-1 hour. The risen dough should spring back when pressed lightly with the fingertip.

5 Turn the dough onto a lightly floured surface, spoon in the rum and knead lightly. Divide the dough into 12 equal-sized pieces, and roll each piece into a ball using the palm of the hand. Place on a greased baking sheet and leave in a warm place for 15 minutes to rise.

6 Heat the oil for deep frying to 375°F. and fry the doughnuts, a few at a time, for 6-8 minutes, turning once, until golden-brown. Remove from the oil with a slotted spoon, draining well, and toss in the sugar. Let cool.

7 Make an incision to the center of each doughnut with a sharp-pointed knife. Make a cone with wax paper and fill with the jam. Cut off the point of the cone and squeeze the jam into the doughnuts.

Makes 12

Dallas Doughnuts

6 tablespoons raspberry jam
1 cup water
1 tablespoon sugar
finely grated rind and juice ½ lemon
1 tablespoon cornstarch
1⅓ cups flour
pinch salt
3 egg yolks
1 tablespoon rum
1 tablespoon sour cream
oil for deep frying
¼ cup confectioners' sugar

1 Place the jam in a pan with the water, sugar, lemon rind and juice. Bring to a boil and simmer for 3 minutes, stirring.

2 Blend the cornstarch with 2 tablespoons water and stir into the pan. Return to a boil, simmer for 1 minute, then remove from the heat.

3 Sift the flour and salt into a bowl. Add the yolks, rum and cream and mix to a smooth dough. Leave for 30 minutes.

4 On a lightly floured surface, roll out the dough to ½ inch thickness. Cut the dough into 2-inch squares with a ravioli cutter or a knife, using a ruler as a guide. Cut 3 incisions through each square to form a 'Y' shape, taking care not to cut through the edge.

5 Heat the oil for deep frying to 375°F. Fry the doughnuts a few at a time for about 3 minutes, until they are golden brown. Drain on absorbent paper. Keep the cooked doughnuts warm.

6 Reheat the jam sauce, strain and serve with the doughnuts.

Serves 4

Apple Doughnuts

German Doughnut recipe
1½ lbs. cooking apples
2 tablespoons water
3 tablespoons sugar
oil for deep frying
sugar for coating

1 Make up the doughnut dough following the instructions in the German Doughnut recipe and, while the dough is rising, prepare the apple filling.

2 Peel, quarter, core and thinly slice the apples. Place them in a pan with the water, cover and bring to a boil. Simmer gently until the apples are soft, shaking the pan occasionally to prevent sticking. Beat the cooked apples until smooth, then cook over high heat for 4-5 minutes to thicken. Stir in the sugar and set aside.

3 Turn out the dough onto a lightly floured surface and knead lightly. Divide into 12 equal-sized pieces and roll each piece into a ball. Flatten each ball into a 4-inch round, and place a heaping teaspoon of the applesauce in the center of each. Bring the edges together, pinching well to seal, and flatten them slightly. Place on a greased baking sheet and leave in a warm place for 15 minutes to rise.

4 Heat the oil for deep frying to 375°F. and fry the doughnuts, a few at a time, for 6-8 minutes, turning once, until golden brown. Remove the cooked doughnuts with a slotted spoon. Drain well, and toss in the sugar. Cool.

5 Serve the doughnuts the same day, since they are best eaten really fresh.

Makes 12

German Doughnuts, crisply fried and filled with jam, are best eaten really fresh. Serve them as a dessert for a tasty change

Custards

Custard is made from a base of milk and egg yolks. It must be cooked gently and stirred frequently to prevent curdling. Once you have perfected the art of making a good custard you can flavor and sweeten it to taste, use it as a filling for pastries and cakes or simply as an accompaniment to your favorite stewed fruit. The following recipes will give you some idea of the many ways you can enhance the simple charm of this underrated dessert.

Crème Brulée

2 tablespoons butter
6 egg yolks
½ cup sugar
2½ cups light cream
3 tablespoons brown sugar

1 Preheat the oven to 300°F. Grease a 3¾-cup shallow ovenproof dish with the butter.

2 In a bowl, cream the egg yolks and sugar. Bring the cream almost to a boil and stir it very gradually into the egg mixture. Strain the custard into the shallow dish. Stand the dish in 1 inch of cold water in a roasting pan and bake in the oven for 1–1½ hours or until the custard has firmly set.

3 Remove the custard from the oven and let it cool. Chill it overnight in the refrigerator.

4 About 1 hour before serving, sprinkle the top with the brown sugar. Brown it very quickly under the broiler, turning the dish occasionally so that the sugar melts evenly. Cool until the sugar topping becomes crisp. Serve with a bowl of whipped cream.

Serves 6

Confectioners' Custard

½ cup flour
4 eggs
⅓ cup sugar
2½ cups milk

1 Sift the flour. Separate the eggs and place the yolks in a bowl — you will not need the whites.

2 Add the sugar to the egg yolks and beat the mixture until it becomes creamy and has increased in bulk. Add the sifted flour all at once and beat in.

3 Bring the milk to a boil in a thick-bottomed saucepan. Gradually whisk the milk into the egg mixture. Return the mixture to the saucepan and bring slowly to a boil, whisking continually. Cook gently until it becomes a smooth cream — the flour will stop it from curdling.

Makes about 3¾ cups

Zuppa Inglese

6 eggs
1⅓ cups sugar
1 tablespoon grated orange rind
⅔ cup flour
⅔ cup cornstarch
1 tablespoon butter
pinch salt

For the Filling:
½ lb. candied fruits
½ cup cherry-flavored liqueur
1¼ cups confectioners' custard

For the Meringue:
3 egg whites
¼ cup sugar
2 tablespoons confectioners' sugar

1 The day before the meal, make the cake. Separate the egg whites from the yolks and place them in separate bowls. Add the sugar to the yolks and beat them until thick and creamy. This should take about 8 minutes of constant beating by hand. Add the orange rind, flour and cornstarch and mix well.

2 Preheat the oven to 325°F. Grease an 8-inch cake pan with the butter.

3 Add a pinch of salt to the egg whites and beat them until they are stiff. Fold the egg whites gently into the cake mixture. Pour the mixture into the cake pan and place it in the oven for 25 minutes. The cake should be just colored when the cooking time is over. Turn the cake out on a rack and cool.

4 On the day of the meal, dice the candied fruits. Place them in a bowl with the liqueur and soak for 2 hours. Drain the fruits, reserving the liquid, and stir them into the confectioners' custard.

5 Cut the cake into 2 layers. Pour half the reserved liquid over each layer. Spread the bottom layer with the confectioners' custard and place the other layer on top.

6 Preheat the oven to 325°F.

7 Prepare the meringue. Beat the egg whites until they start to whiten. Add the sugar and continue beating until stiff. Cover the cake with large swirls of the meringue, using a decorators' bag or large spoon. Sprinkle the meringue with the confectioners' sugar.

8 Place the cake on the top shelf of the oven for 6-8 minutes to lightly brown the meringue. Remove from the oven and allow to cool. Chill in the refrigerator and serve.

Serves 6–8

Look 'n Cook Confectioners' Custard

1 Separate the eggs and place the yolks in a bowl. You will not need the whites **2** Add the sugar to the yolks and whisk until they are creamy **3** Whisk in the sifted flour **4** Bring the milk to a boil, whisking occasionally to stop a skin from forming **5** Gradually whisk it into the egg mixture **6** Return the custard to the saucepan and whisk gently over low heat until it is smooth

Basic Baked Egg Custard

2¼ cups milk
3 eggs
2 tablespoons sugar
1 teaspoon grated nutmeg

1 Preheat the oven to 325°F.

2 Heat the milk gently in a saucepan. Make sure that it does not boil.

3 Meanwhile, beat the eggs and sugar together in a mixing bowl.

4 Pour in the hot milk, stirring continuously. Then pour the custard into a greased ovenproof dish and sprinkle on the grated nutmeg.

5 Place the dish in the preheated oven and bake until set (about 45 minutes).

Serves 4

Pear and Almond Custard

4 pears, peeled, cored and
  quartered
1¼ cups water
⅔ cups sugar
⅓ cup blanched almonds
few drops almond extract
2 egg yolks
3 tablespoons cornstarch
1¼ cups light cream
4 candied cherries
1 tablespoon sliced almonds

1 Place the pears, water and sugar together in a saucepan and bring to a boil. Poach until the pears are tender.

2 Strain off the syrup and purée

Pear and Almond Custard tastes as good as it looks with its fresh juicy pears in a delicately flavored almond custard

with the blanched almonds and almond extract.

3 Blend the egg yolks, cornstarch and 2 tablespoons of the cream together in a bowl. Then stir in the syrup and the rest of the cream.

4 Reheat in a saucepan just to boiling point, then allow to cool.

5 Divide the pears between four attractive glasses and pour in the almond custard.

6 Decorate with candied cherries and sliced almonds. Chill before serving.

Serves 4

Tips: If fresh pears are out of season or unavailable, you can always substitute canned pears.

To blanch almonds, just pour boiling water over them and leave for a few minutes. Remove the skins by squeezing the end of each nut — the almond will pop out.

Baked Custard Tarts

dough for one 9-inch pie crust
butter
$1\frac{3}{4}$ cups milk
$\frac{1}{2}$ teaspoon vanilla extract
3 eggs
1 tablespoon sugar
1 teaspoon grated nutmeg

1 Preheat the oven to 400°F.

2 Roll out the dough $\frac{1}{8}$ inch thick. Butter some tartlet tins and line with the dough. Prick the bottoms and put aside in a cool place.

3 Place the milk and vanilla extract in a saucepan and heat through.

4 Meanwhile, cream together the eggs and sugar until light and creamy. Pour on the hot milk, stirring well, and then strain. Cool.

5 When cool, pour the custard into the prepared tartlet tins. Leave about $\frac{1}{4}$ inch at the top of each tin.

6 Sprinkle the tarts with grated nutmeg and bake in the oven for about 20 minutes until cooked and golden. Serve cold with cream.

Serves 4–6

Tips: You can flavor these delicious tarts with a few drops of your favorite liqueur — orange liqueurs are particularly good. Or add some instant coffee granules or cocoa. Another idea is to stir some chestnut purée into the custard mixture.

Also, be careful not to overcook these tarts. As soon as the custard rises and feels firm, the tarts are cooked. It is easy to overcook and allow them to become watery. It helps if you place the tartlet tins on a hot baking sheet in the oven.

Floating Islands with Oranges — egg whites floating on top of a creamy custard which is flavored with oranges

Floating Islands with Oranges

4 eggs, separated
pinch salt
1 cup sugar
$2\frac{1}{4}$ cups milk
2 oranges
$\frac{1}{4}$ cup orange-flavored liqueur

1 Beat the egg whites with a pinch of salt until they form stiff peaks. Beat in $\frac{1}{2}$ cup of the sugar, a little at a time.

2 Bring water to a boil and drop the meringue, a few tablespoonfuls at a time, into the water. Simmer for about 10 minutes until cooked through. Remove, drain and dry on a clean cloth. Repeat until all the meringue is used up.

3 Meanwhile, heat the milk and grate the rind and squeeze the juice of 1 orange. Add the grated rind to the milk.

4 Cream together the egg yolks with the remaining sugar and gradually whisk in the hot milk away from the heat. When all the milk is added, return the mixture to the saucepan and gently reheat, stirring all the time, until the custard is thick and coats the back of a spoon. Cool a little, then stir in the orange juice and liqueur. Pour into a serving dish.

5 With a zesting knife, make vertical grooves at regular intervals around the remaining orange. Then slice it thinly, horizontally. Decorate the top of the custard with the meringues and arrange the slices of orange around the sides of the dish to form an attractive border.

Serves 4

Tip: As a variation on this dish, you can stretch it further by pouring the orange custard onto a layer of sponge cake soaked in sherry, or crushed macaroons sprinkled with an orange-flavored liqueur.

Another way of cooking the whisked egg white meringue is to drop the spoonfuls into the hot milk which you intend to use for the custard.

Look 'n Cook Floating Islands

1 and **2** Separate the eggs and place the yolks and whites in different bowls **3** Add half the sugar to the egg yolks and whisk them to a cream **4** and **5** Whisk the egg whites until stiff, add the remaining sugar and continue to whisk until they are very stiff **6** Heat the milk and vanilla extract in a large saucepan. Drop 4 tablespoonfuls of the meringue into the hot (not boiling) milk and poach them for 5 minutes on either side

7 Remove and place them to drain on a clean cloth
8 Bring the milk to a boil and gradually whisk it into
the egg yolks 9 and 10 Return the custard to the
saucepan and cook it gently, stirring continually, until
it coats the spoon 11 and 12 Strain it and pour it
into 4 individual serving dishes. Let it cool. Place a
poached meringue on top, chill and serve

Floating Islands

5 eggs
⅔ cup sugar
3 cups milk
½ teaspoon vanilla extract

1 Break the eggs and place the whites and yolks in separate bowls.

2 Add half the sugar to the yolks and beat them until they are creamy. Beat the egg whites until they are stiff, add the remaining sugar and continue to beat until the meringue is very stiff.

3 Bring the milk and vanilla to a boil, reduce the heat and drop 4 tablespoonfuls of the meringue mixture into the saucepan. Let the meringues poach for 5 minutes on either side. Remove them with a slotted spoon and place them on a clean cloth to dry.

4 Return the milk to a boil and gradually whisk it into the egg yolk mixture. Return this mixture to the saucepan and cook it over low heat, stirring constantly with a wooden spoon until the custard is smooth and coats the spoon.

5 Strain the custard and pour it into 4 individual serving dishes. Allow the custard to cool. Place a poached meringue on top of each dish and chill in the refrigerator for 1 hour before serving.

Serves 4

Almond Coffee Cream

2 eggs
⅔ cup sugar
1 cup heavy cream
¾ cup almonds
¼ cup cold black coffee
¾ cup confectioners' sugar

Almond Coffee Cream is a smooth, rich dessert, topped with almonds and garnished with rich coffee-flavored candies

For the Garnish:
24 coffee-flavored candies

1 Separate the eggs and place the yolks in a bowl. You will not need the whites.

2 Place the bowl containing the egg yolks in a bowl of hot, but not boiling, water. Add the sugar to the yolks and beat the mixture thoroughly for 3 minutes. Gradually pour in ¼ cup of the cream and continue to beat until the mixture is thick and smooth.

3 Preheat the oven to 400°F. Place the almonds in a small saucepan with just enough water to cover them. Bring the water to a boil and remove the saucepan from the heat. Drain and rinse the almonds and peel off their skins. Chop them into

978

fine slivers. Wrap them in aluminum foil and place in the preheated oven for 2 minutes. Allow them to cool in the foil.

4 Reserve 1 tablespoon of the almond slivers and mix the rest into the egg mixture.

5 Whip the remaining cream and stir in the black coffee. Gently fold in the confectioners' sugar. Mix this coffee cream with the egg yolk mixture.

6 Pour the cream into 4 individual serving dishes. Place them in the refrigerator to chill for at least 4 hours. Sprinkle with the reserved almonds, garnish with the coffee-flavored candies and serve.

Serves 4

Cabinet Pudding

one plain 8-inch sponge cake
⅓ cup candied cherries
2 tablespoons angelica
1 tablespoon butter
1 tablespoon sugar

For the Custard:
3 eggs
¼ cup sugar
½ teaspoon vanilla extract
2¼ cups milk

1 Cut the sponge cake into ½-inch cubes and place them in a bowl. Quarter the cherries and cut the angelica into small strips. Carefully

---

Cabinet Pudding, a traditional British dessert, is a tasty mixture of sponge cake and candied fruits set in an egg custard

mix them both with the cake cubes.

2 Butter the inside of six ⅔-cup molds and sprinkle each with a little sugar. Divide the cake mixture between the 6 molds. Preheat the oven to 400°F.

3 Prepare the custard. In a bowl, cream together the eggs, sugar and vanilla extract. Heat the milk without letting it boil and blend it thoroughly with the egg mixture. Pass the custard through a strainer and divide it between each of the 6 molds. Allow 30 minutes for the custard to soak through the cake.

4 Place the molds in a roasting pan with 1½ inches of water. Bake them in the oven for 30 minutes or until they are set. Turn them out onto a serving dish and serve immediately with a bowl of whipped cream.

Serves 6

Papaya Orange Custard

1½ cups milk
1 tablespoon cornstarch
2 tablespoons sugar
1 egg, beaten
½ cup orange juice
few drops lemon extract
1 cup mashed papayas
4 candied cherries

1 Place the milk in a saucepan and bring to a boil.

2 Meanwhile, mix together the cornstarch, sugar, beaten egg and a little of the orange juice. Blend well together.

3 Pour into the boiling milk and cook for 1 minute, stirring all the time. Remove from the heat and allow to cool a little.

4 Stir in the rest of the orange juice and a few drops of lemon extract. Then add the mashed papaya and pour the custard into individual attractive glasses. Chill in the refrigerator.

5 Decorate each glass with a candied cherry before serving.

Serves 4

Tips: If you have difficulty finding papayas, you can substitute other fruit in this delicious custard. Try chopped orange or tangerine, fresh chopped apricots or peaches, and even raspberries or strawberries. You can also utilize the canned fruit in your cupboard, such as mandarin oranges and pineapple chunks.

Papaya Orange Custard, flavored with orange juice and the tropical tang of crushed papayas, is topped with a candied cherry

Grape Custard

2¼ cups sweet white wine
grated rind 1 lemon
6 egg yolks
¾ cup sugar
3 tablespoons cornstarch
3 tablespoons water
4 egg whites
pinch salt
juice 1 lemon
½ lb. green grapes
½ lb. purple grapes
¼ cup brandy

For the Garnish:
2 egg whites
¼ cup sugar

1 Boil the white wine and lemon rind for 2 minutes.

2 Blend the egg yolks with half of the sugar. Mix in the cornstarch and water.

3 Gradually stir in the hot wine, then pour back into the saucepan and bring to a boil, stirring until thick. Remove from the heat.

4 Beat the egg whites and salt until they form stiff peaks. Add the rest of the sugar and beat until thick. Fold into the warm custard with the lemon juice.

5 Reserve 18 green and purple grapes for decoration. Halve and seed the remaining grapes. Marinate them in the brandy.

6 Beat the egg whites for the garnish and dip the rims of 6 tall glasses into the mixture. Then dip into sugar.

7 Dip the grapes into the beaten egg whites and sugar, and chill.

8 Divide the grapes between the glasses. Top up with the custard mixture and chill for 2 hours. Decorate with the grapes.

Serves 6

Grape Custard, chilled and served with frosted grapes, is a rich and nutritious dessert with a smooth and creamy texture

Look 'n Cook Whisky Sabayon

1 The ingredients **2** Whisk together the egg yolks, sugar and nutmeg. Add the whisky and heat over a pan of hot water until the mixture is thick **3** Add the orange and lemon juice and continue to whisk over the pan of hot water until the mixture is thick and pale. Remove the bowl from the heat and whisk until the mixture is cool **4** Spoon the mixture into 4 glasses. Decorate with grated orange rind

Coffee Banana Custard

3 eggs
2 tablespoons sugar
1 tablespoon instant coffee
  granules
2¼ cups milk
2 bananas
grated chocolate to decorate

1 Beat together the eggs, sugar and coffee. Warm the milk and pour into the egg mixture, stirring well.

2 Strain the mixture into a heavy-based pan and stir over gentle heat with a wooden spoon until the custard thinly coats the back of the spoon. Do not allow it to boil. Cool slightly.

3 Slice the bananas thinly and divide between 4 individual glass serving dishes.

4 Pour the warm coffee custard over the bananas and sprinkle the tops with grated chocolate. Serve immediately.

Serves 4

Tip: Orange Strawberry custard can be made following the recipe above. Omit the instant coffee granules and grated chocolate from the ingredients. Put a few strips of thinly pared orange rind in the milk when it is warmed, cover the pan and let it infuse for 10 minutes before pouring into the egg mixture. Slice some fresh strawberries into the serving dishes and decorate the tops with finely grated orange rind.

Whisky Sabayon

6 egg yolks
¾ cup sugar
pinch grated nutmeg
⅓ cup whisky
juice 1 lemon
grated rind and juice 1 orange

1 Beat together the egg yolks, sugar and nutmeg in a large bowl.

2 Add the whisky, place the bowl over a pan of hot water and beat until the mixture is thick.

3 Add the lemon and orange juice and continue to beat over the pan of hot water until the mixture is thick and pale.

4 Remove the bowl from the heat and beat until the mixture is cool. Spoon into 4 individual glass serving dishes, and decorate each with a little grated orange rind. Serve chilled.

Serves 4

Pear Brioche — yeasty, rich brioche stuffed with fresh chopped pears, crisp macaroons and cherry-flavored custard

Pear Brioche

3¾ cups flour
1 teaspoon salt
1½ tablespoons fresh yeast
3 tablespoons sugar
⅓ cup milk
2 eggs, beaten
¼ cup butter

For the Filling:
3 egg yolks
1 whole egg
½ cup flour
⅓ cup sugar
2¼ cups milk
2 tablespoons cherry-flavored
  liqueur

4 ripe pears
6 almond macaroons, crushed
½ cup apricot jam

1 For the brioche: sift the flour and salt into a warm bowl. Blend the yeast with 1 teaspoon of the sugar, and add to the flour with the milk, beaten eggs, and the remaining sugar. Beat well until the dough is smooth and elastic. Work the butter into the dough.

2 Cover the bowl with a damp cloth and let rise in a warm place for 40 minutes. Preheat the oven to 425°F.

3 Stir the dough well and turn into a lightly greased Charlotte mold or cake pan. Cover and leave to rise for 15 minutes.

4 Bake for 50 minutes, until golden brown. Turn out onto a wire rack to cool.

5 For the filling: place the egg yolks, whole egg, flour and sugar in a bowl and mix together well. Heat the milk and pour into the egg mixture, stirring. Return the mixture to the pan and stir continuously over medium heat until the mixture comes to a boil. Remove from the

---

Lemon Sabayon is a smooth and creamy custard dessert made with fresh lemons, orange liqueur, egg yolks, sugar and milk

heat immediately, add the liqueur and cool.

6 Peel, core and dice the pears. Stir the pears and crushed macaroons into the cooled custard.

7 Turn the oven to 375°F. Remove a slice from the top of the brioche and scoop out some of the inside, leaving a hole almost large enough to hold the pear custard. Wrap the brioche loosely in aluminum foil and place in the oven for about 15 minutes to warm through.

8 Meanwhile, melt the apricot jam in a pan with 2 tablespoons water. Gently reheat the pear custard.

9 Stand the brioche on a heated serving dish and pour on the melted jam, coating the inside generously, and allowing a little to drizzle down the outside. Fill the brioche with the heated pear custard and serve immediately.

Serves 6

Lemon Sabayon

4 egg yolks
1 whole egg
¼ cup sugar
finely grated rind and juice 1 lemon
1 tablespoon orange-flavored liqueur
1¼ cups sweet vermouth

1 Place the egg yolks, whole egg and sugar together in a bowl and beat for 5 minutes.

2 Beat in the lemon rind and juice, liqueur and vermouth.

3 Place the bowl over a pan of hot water and continue to beat until the mixture is thick and pale.

4 Remove the bowl from the heat and beat until the mixture is cool. Spoon into 4 individual glass dishes and serve chilled.

Serves 4

Queen of Puddings

2¼ cups milk
¾ cup sugar
4 cups cake crumbs
grated rind 2 lemons
2 eggs, separated
¾ cup apricot jam

1 Preheat the oven to 350°F. Heat the milk and ¼ cup of the sugar gently in a saucepan. Stir in the cake crumbs and lemon rind and remove from the heat. Beat in the egg yolks.

2 Pour half the mixture into a buttered earthenware dish and bake it in the oven for 30 minutes or until set.

3 Heat the apricot jam in a saucepan and spread half over the top of the set custard. Fill up the dish with the remaining egg yolk mixture and return it to the oven for a further 30 minutes or until it is thoroughly set.

4 Cover the top of the pudding with the rest of the jam. Beat the egg whites with ⅓ cup of the remaining sugar until stiff.

5 Raise the oven temperature to 375°F. Spoon the meringue onto the pudding and sprinkle with the remaining sugar. Return to the oven and bake for 5 minutes or until the meringue is golden. Serve immediately.

Serves 6

Crème Caramel

2 tablespoons water
½ cup sugar

Crème Caramel is a classic French dessert which is always a favorite at parties with its creamy texture and caramel topping

4 eggs
¼ cup sugar
½ teaspoon vanilla extract
2¼ cups milk

1 Make the caramel. Bring half of the water and ½ cup sugar to a boil in a heavy-based saucepan. When it begins to caramelize, add the remaining water and reboil until the water and caramel mix.

2 Line the mold as shown on the opposite page.

3 Preheat the oven to 350°F. Cream together the eggs, sugar and vanilla extract. Heat the milk, without letting it boil, and gradually blend it into the egg mixture. Strain this cream and pour it into the mold. Place the mold in a roasting pan, half-filled with water, and bake for 1 hour, or until set.

4 Chill thoroughly before turning out the caramel onto a serving dish. Pour any caramel remaining in the mold around the dish and serve.

Serves 6

Look 'n Cook Lining a Crème Caramel Mold

1 Hold the rim of the mold with a clean cloth to prevent burning your hands and pour in the caramel 2 and 3 Tip and rotate the mold so the base is covered in caramel 4 and 5 Tip the mold so it is almost on its side and continue to rotate it until all the sides are well coated 6 When the interior of the mold is completely coated, pour off and discard the excess caramel

Rice Desserts

Rice pudding is not a name that conjures visions of exotic culinary delights; for many people it is a reminder of institutional cooking that they prefer to forget. However, rice pudding is not only easy, cheap and nutritious — it can also be delicious and impressive. Even a basic rice pudding can be varied in many ways. Try adding beaten egg, spices, raisins, chopped candied fruits, or cream. Serve it with unusual fruits such as mango, papaya or passion fruit.

Basic Rice Pudding

¼ cup short grain rice
2 tablespoons butter
2 tablespoons sugar
2¼ cups milk
pinch grated nutmeg

1 Preheat the oven to 300°F.

2 Wash the rice in a colander under running water, and drain. Butter an ovenproof dish.

3 Place the rice and sugar in the dish. Pour in the milk and top with the rest of the butter, cut in small pieces. Dust with freshly grated nutmeg.

4 Bake in the oven for 2 hours, stirring the pudding after ½ hour. Serve hot or cold.

Serves 4

Banana Rice Caramel

½ cup short grain rice
3⅔ cups milk
1 cup sugar
1 tablespoon water
4 bananas
½ teaspoon vanilla extract
4 eggs, beaten

1 Place the rice in a pan of cold water and bring it to a boil. Rinse with cold water and drain.

2 Bring the milk to a boil in a pan and add the rice. Cook for about 40 minutes until the rice is very tender and has absorbed the milk.

Banana Rice Caramel is served either hot or cold. Your children will adore the flavor of the bananas and sticky toffee

3 Meanwhile, make the caramel by melting ½ cup sugar in the water, stirring constantly. Boil to 315°F. when it starts to color. Remove the pan from the heat and dip its base at once into cold water to stop the sugar from cooking further.

4 Pour the caramel into a mold. Holding the mold with a cloth, turn it so that the caramel is distributed over the sides. Allow the caramel to cool to a sticky consistency.

5 Preheat the oven to 350°F. Peel and slice 3 bananas. Arrange the slices over the bottom of the mold and in one row around the sides.

6 When the rice is cooked, stir in ½ cup sugar and the vanilla extract. Fold in the beaten eggs. Pour the mixture into the mold lined with caramel and banana.

7 Bake the rice in a pan of water in the oven for 40 minutes. Turn out the mold onto a serving dish. Peel and slice the remaining banana and arrange the slices around the pudding. Serve hot or cold.

Serves 4-6

Mandarin Condé is a substantial dessert — the tangy flavor of mandarin oranges provide a contrast to the creamy rice

Mandarin Condé

⅓ cup rice
2¼ cups milk
¼ cup sugar
½ teaspoon vanilla extract
1 tablespoon candied orange peel
  cut in small strips
1 cup canned mandarin orange
  sections
½ cup candied cherries

For the Apricot Glaze:
¼ cup apricot jam
2 tablespoons sugar
1¼ cups water

2 teaspoons cornstarch
1 tablespoon orange-flavored
  liqueur

1 Place the rice in a pan of cold water. Bring to a boil. Rinse in cold water.

2 Bring the milk to a boil in a pan. Add the rice and cook until it is soft and has absorbed the milk.

3 Stir in the sugar and vanilla extract and add the pieces of candied orange peel. Moisten a mold and pour the rice into it. Press it down level and firmly, and let it cool.

4 To make the apricot glaze, heat the jam, sugar and water gently un-til they are melted and smooth. Add the cornstarch, dissolved in a little water, and boil for 2 minutes until the glaze clears. Stir in the liqueur.

5 When the rice is cold and set, turn it out onto a serving dish. Arrange the mandarin sections on top of and around, the rice. Place a whole cherry in the middle and halved cherries in the mandarin sections around the rice. Pour the apricot glaze over the middle of the rice so that it flows down the sides. Serve cold.

Serves 4-6

Tip: Many different orange liqueurs may be used to flavor the apricot glaze. Or the liqueur can be replaced by orange extract, but this is much stronger, so use only 2-3 drops.

Look 'n Cook Rice Condé with Apricots

1 Place the rice in a saucepan of cold water and bring it to a boil **2** Rinse the rice in cold water and leave it until it is quite cold **3** Drain the rice through a colander **4** Bring the milk to a boil and pour the rice into it **5** Br-ing the mixture back to a boil, then cover the pan and place it in a preheated oven. Bake for about 40 minutes until the rice is completely cooked **6** Add the vanilla extract and mix well **7** Gently stir in the sugar **8**

Dampen a shallow cake pan. Pour the rice into it and press it down firmly and evenly **9** Allow the rice to cool. Turn it out onto a serving dish **10** Decorate the top with the apricot halves **11** Glaze the top of the fruit with the apricot glaze **12** Decorate the dish with candied cherries and angelica

Rice Condé with Apricots

½ cup short or long grain rice
3 cups milk
½ teaspoon vanilla extract
½ cup sugar
¼ cup apricot jam
2 teaspoons cherry-flavored liqueur
12 canned apricot halves
6 candied cherries
1 stick candied angelica

1 Preheat the oven to 325°F.

2 Place the rice in a saucepan of cold water and bring to a boil. Drain, rinse in cold water, and drain again through a colander.

3 In an ovenproof pan or casserole, bring the milk to a boil. Add the rice and bring it back to a boil. Cover the pan or casserole and place it in the oven. Cook for 1 hour or until the rice has absorbed all the milk.

4 Remove the rice from the oven. Gently stir in the vanilla extract (do not add too much) and the sugar with a fork.

5 Moisten a shallow cake pan with cold water and pour the rice into it. Press it down firmly and make an even flat surface. Let cool.

6 Melt the apricot jam in a pan over low heat and stir in the liqueur.

7 Place a serving dish over the rice mold and turn it over so that the rice comes out of the pan in one piece. Arrange the canned apricot halves over the top and pour the melted apricot glaze over them. Decorate with the cherries and the candied angelica, cut in short strips. Serve cold.

Serves 4–6

Tip: Do not add sugar to the milk while it is cooking, as this will prevent the rice from swelling up. You could substitute other fruit for the apricots in this recipe: try using peaches, pears or cherries.

Empress Rice Pudding

3 cups milk
⅓ cup short grain rice
½ cup sugar
½ teaspoon vanilla extract
¼ cup unflavored gelatin
¼ cup diced mixed candied fruit and peel
⅔ cup all-purpose cream
2 egg whites
9 candied cherries to garnish

1 In a saucepan, bring the milk to a boil. Wash the rice and add it to the

Empress Rice Pudding is a creamy and colorful dessert, and is decorated with delicious diced candied fruits and mixed peel

milk. Simmer until the rice is tender and has absorbed the milk.

2 Stir the sugar gently into the rice. Blend in the vanilla extract.

3 Dissolve the gelatin in a little hot water. Cool and add to the rice. Add the diced candied fruit and peel, and mix well.

4 Cool. Beat the cream lightly and fold it into the rice.

5 Beat the egg whites until stiff. Fold them into the rice. Moisten a ring mold with cold water and pour the rice mixture into it. Place the mold in the refrigerator and chill until the mixture is firmly set.

6 Turn the rice pudding out onto a serving dish. Place the cherries around the top to decorate and serve.

Serves 4–6

All about Cheesecakes, Sponge Desserts and Meringues

Apricot Cheesecake

Cheesecakes

Cheesecakes are becoming increasingly popular and you can easily make your own at home. They can be baked or set with gelatin. They are nearly always served cold. There is a wide range of attractive and delicious cheesecake recipes to choose from. They may be made with cream, cottage or ricotta cheese on a base of rich crust or cookie crumbs.

You can top cheesecakes with whipped cream, fresh or candied fruit, or a fruit glaze. You can sprinkle a layer of fresh fruit, such as raspberries; or dried fruits between the crust and the cheesecake mixture. Cream and cottage cheese have rather a bland flavor, therefore the grated rind and juice of a lemon or orange are often added. In Italy, grated Parmesan cheese is sometimes mixed into the cheesecake for extra flavor.

Cheesecakes freeze particularly well so you can make one in advance, freeze it until you need it, and decorate just before serving with fruit, cream or a glaze.

Pineapple Cheesecake

1¼ cups gingersnap crumbs
¼ lb. butter
4 ozs. cream cheese
½ cup crushed pineapple
¼ cup sugar
1 tablespoon lemon juice
¼ cup water
2 tablespoons unflavored gelatin

⅔ cup heavy cream
4 pineapple rings
6 candied cherries
angelica to decorate

1 Crush the gingersnaps. This is best done by placing them in a paper bag. Secure the end and crush with a heavy rolling pin.

2 Place the crushed cookies in a bowl. Heat the butter in a saucepan and mix well with the melted butter.

3 Spread the cookie mixture over the base of an 8-inch diameter shallow springform pan.

4 Blend together the cream cheese, crushed pineapple and sugar. Stir in the lemon juice.

5 Warm the water and dissolve the gelatin. Stir well until it is dissolved. Cool a little, then add to the cream cheese mixture.

6 Whip the cream until stiff and fold in with a metal spoon. Pour the cheesecake mixture over the crust base and level off the top. Chill in the refrigerator for about 3 hours until firm and set.

7 Remove the cheesecake from the mold and place on an attractive serving plate.

8 Cut the pineapple rings into chunks and slice the cherries in half. Slice the angelica to make two thin 'stems' and four diamond-shaped 'leaves.'

9 Next, make two flowers using the pineapple chunks as 'petals,' the cherries as centers and angelica 'stems' and 'leaves.' Arrange these flowers on the top of the cheesecake. Place the remaining pineapple and cherries alternately around the base to form a decorative border.

Serves 6

Tips: You can use cottage cheese instead of cream cheese in this recipe. To give it a more lemony, sharper flavor, add a little grated lemon rind.

Chocolate Orange Cheesecake

1¼ cups graham cracker crumbs
¼ lb. butter
pinch cinnamon
butter for greasing
¼ cup milk
3 ozs. semisweet chocolate
8 ozs. cream cheese
¼ cup water
4 tablespoons unflavored gelatin
juice and grated rind 1 orange
⅔ cup heavy cream, whipped
3 candied cherries
chocolate wafer candies to
  decorate

1 Crush the graham crackers as described above. Melt the butter and blend with the crumbs and cinnamon.

2 Butter the bottom of an 8-inch springform pan and line the sides with wax paper.

3 Spread the crumb mixture over the base of the pan.

4 Place the milk and chocolate in a saucepan and heat gently, stirring until the chocolate melts. Mix well with the cream cheese.

5 Heat the water and dissolve the gelatin. Reheat until you have a clear jelly-like substance.

6 Stir the gelatin into the cream cheese and the orange rind and juice. Fold in the whipped cream, and then pour the mixture into the pan.

7 Chill in the refrigerator for 3 hours until set and firm. Remove the cheesecake from the pan and place on a serving plate. Decorate the top with halved cherries and chocolate wafers before serving.

Serves 6–8

Pineapple Cheesecake (top) and Chocolate Orange Cheesecake (below) are good to look at and great to eat

Red Currant Cheesecake

6 tablespoons butter
3 tablespoons honey
6 cups cornflakes
2 eggs, separated
$\frac{1}{4}$ cup sugar
8 ozs. cream cheese
$\frac{1}{4}$ cup lemon juice
2 tablespoons water
2 tablespoons unflavored gelatin
$\frac{2}{3}$ cup heavy cream
2 cups red currants
$\frac{1}{4}$ cup melted red currant jelly

1 Preheat the oven to 350°F.

2 In a saucepan, melt the butter and honey together. Stir in the cornflakes until they are well coated. Press the mixture around the base of a lightly buttered, 8-inch springform pan. Bake for 10 minutes. Cool.

3 Cream the egg yolks with the sugar in a bowl. Beat in the cream cheese. Add the lemon juice gradually, and beat until soft and smooth.

4 Heat the water and melt the gelatin in it. Add this to the cheese mixture and stir until well blended. Allow to cool almost to setting point.

5 In separate bowls, beat the egg whites and the heavy cream until they are both stiff. Gradually fold the cream into the cheese mixture. Then gently fold in the beaten egg whites.

6 Pour the mixture in the crust and allow it to set. When set, remove the ring and slide the cheesecake onto a serving dish.

7 Wash and pick over the red currants (if they are not very ripe, cook them for 5 minutes in a little water and sugar, then drain). Arrange them over the top of the cheesecake and cover with the melted red currant jelly. Serve cold.

Serves 6

Red Currant Cheesecake has a smooth, creamy texture and is topped with a colorful and fruity fresh red currant glaze

Apple and Raisin Cheesecake

one 8-inch pie crust
2 sweet apples
$\frac{1}{4}$ cup butter
1 egg
$\frac{1}{4}$ cup sugar
2 tablespoons flour
5 ozs. cream cheese

¼ cup light cream
2 drops vanilla extract
⅓ cup raisins
⅔ cup all-purpose cream

1 Preheat the oven to 400°F. Roll the dough on a floured board to ¼ inch thick. Lightly butter a flan ring and line it with the dough. Prick the bottom and bake for 10-15 minutes.

2 Meanwhile, peel, core and thinly slice the apples. Melt the butter in a pan and cook the apple slices over gentle heat for a few minutes until tender. Strain and allow to cool.

3 To make the cheesecake filling, beat the egg with the sugar. Blend in the flour. Add the cream cheese and beat until soft. Gradually beat in the cream and vanilla extract. Finally, fold in the raisins.

4 Remove the crust from the oven and lower the oven temperature to 375°F. Let the crust cool and then

Apple and Raisin Cheesecake is layered with fruit to help make it light and moist, and is garnished with whipped cream

pour in half the cheesecake mixture. Cover it with a layer of apple slices. Pour the rest of the mixture over the top. Bake for 30 minutes.

5 Beat the all-purpose cream until stiff. Remove the cheesecake from the oven and remove the ring. When it is cool, top with whipped cream and serve.

Serves 6

Tip: To give the apple slices a delicious flavor, cook them with 1 teaspoon powdered cinnamon. Other seasonal fruits, such as plums or pears, could be substituted for the apples.

Mock Cheesecake

1½ cups cookie crumbs
2 tablespoons sugar
¼ cup butter, melted
4 eggs, separated
1¼ cups sweetened condensed milk
grated rind and juice 2 lemons

1 Preheat the oven to 375°F. In a mixing bowl blend the cookie crumbs, sugar and melted butter. Line a springform pan with the mixture.

2 Beat the egg yolks. Stir in the condensed milk, lemon rind and juice. Beat the egg whites until stiff. Fold the whites into the mixture and pour it into the crust. Bake for 15-20 minutes in the preheated oven, cool and serve.

Serves 6

Apricot Cheesecake

15 ozs. canned apricots in syrup
1 package orange gelatin
1 lb. cottage cheese
2 tablespoons sugar
⅔ cup heavy cream, whipped
1 cup gingersnap crumbs
2 tablespoons brown sugar
¼ cup butter, melted

For the Decoration:
2 tablespoons apricot jam
15 ozs. canned apricots in syrup
2 tablespoons sliced almonds

1 Make up the syrup from the canned apricots to 1¼ cups with water. Bring to a boil, add the gelatin and stir to dissolve. Cool.

2 Purée the apricots and cheese and stir in the cooled gelatin and sugar. Fold in the cream.

3 Line the base of an 8-inch springform pan with wax paper. Pour in the mixture and chill to set.

4 Combine the crumbs, brown sugar and butter, sprinkle over the set mixture and press down with a spoon.

5 Melt the jam with 1 tablespoon of the apricot syrup, strain and cool. Turn out the cheesecake and decorate with the apricots. Brush with the jam glaze and sprinkle with almonds.

Serves 8

Avocado Orange Cheesecake

1¼ cups cookie crumbs
¼ cup butter, melted
1 avocado

¼ cup lemon juice
3 ozs. cream cheese
⅔ cup sour cream
1 orange
2 tablespoons sugar
1½ teaspoons unflavored gelatin
  dissolved in 1 tablespoon water
1 egg white

1 Mix the crumbs with the butter, and press the mixture evenly into the base of a lightly greased flan pan. Place in the refrigerator and chill until set.

2 Peel, pit and mash ¾ of the

Avocado Orange Cheesecake has a deliciously unusual flavor, and would be the perfect choice for a summer buffet

avocado. Thinly slice the remaining ¼ and dip the slices in lemon juice; reserve for garnish.

3 Beat the cream cheese, sour cream, and remaining lemon juice into the mashed avocado. Grate the rind of ½ the orange and add. Stir in the sugar.

4 Combine the gelatin with the avocado mixture. Beat the egg white until stiff and fold in.

5 Pour the mixture into the crumb crust and chill until set. Remove the flan from the ring. Peel and slice the rest of the orange, and decorate the top of the cheesecake with orange slices and the reserved avocado slices.

Serves 6

Trifles

The dictionary defines a 'trifle' as a paltry, insignificant thing; and as a dessert. A classic trifle dessert, however, is far from insignificant. At its best it is light but lavish, somewhat alcoholic and highly decorative. The trifle was developed in Great Britain in the eighteenth century, from the Elizabethan dish of syllabub. A trifle should have four layers: the first of sponge cakes soaked in sherry and fruit juice; then a layer of fruit; then one of custard, and a topping of whipped cream. The modern, less rich and filling versions often substitute flavored gelatin for one of these layers, and do not include sherry. Whatever the layers contain, trifles are easy and popular with old and young alike.

Country Trifles

2 ozs. raspberry gelatin
1 cup canned fruit cocktail with syrup
½ cup granola
2 tablespoons powdered custard mix
2 tablespoons sugar
2 cups milk

For the Topping:
⅔ cup heavy cream
2 tablespoons granola
2 candied cherries

1 In a pan dissolve the gelatin in ⅔ cup boiling water. Stir in the syrup from the can of fruit cocktail. Measure the liquid and make it up to 1¼ cups with cold water.

2 Divide the fruit salad and the granola between four single-serving sundae glasses. Pour the gelatin into the glasses. Leave them in a cool place or in the refrigerator until set.

3 Mix the custard powder with the sugar and ¼ cup of the milk in a bowl, until smooth. Heat the rest of the milk in a pan until almost boiling. Stir in the custard powder mixture and return the pan to the heat, stirring while the custard comes to a boil. Cook for 1 minute, stirring constantly. Remove the pan from the heat. Cover the custard while it cools. Leave until almost cold.

4 When the custard is nearly set, pour it over the gelatin in the sun-

Country Trifles — delicious layers of granola, fruit salad, gelatin and custard, topped with rosettes of cream

dae glasses. Spread it level and chill until the custard is firm.

5 Whip the cream until stiff and place it in a decorator's bag. Pipe the cream in rosettes around the edge of the custard. Place the granola for the topping inside the cream border in each glass. Put a candied cherry on top of each trifle and serve cold.

Serves 4

Tip: To vary the trifles, you could arrange mandarin orange sections over the top and perhaps sprinkle a little orange-flavored liqueur over the fruit before adding the gelatin. Allow 1 teaspoon of the liqueur per portion.

1 The ingredients: sponge cake, sherry, brandy, eggs, milk, jam, almond-flavored cookies, candied fruits and almonds **2** Split the sponge cakes and spread with raspberry jam. Sandwich them together and cut into squares **3** Place the cake squares, cookies and sliced almonds in a glass bowl. Mix the sherry, brandy and extracts (optional) and pour over the cake **4** In a bowl combine the egg yolks, cornstarch and a little milk. Pour in the boiling milk and stir. Return to the pan and reheat until thickened **5** Pour the custard over the cakes and leave in a cool place to set **6** Whip the cream until stiff and spread it over the set custard. Make a swirling pattern on it and decorate with candied cherries and strips of candied angelica **7** The finished dish should be served cold. Almonds may also be used to decorate the top

Christmas Cake Trifle

½–¾ lb. leftover Christmas or fruit
cake
2 tablespoons brandy
1 lb. ripe pears
2¼ cups custard
⅔ cup all-purpose cream

1 Cut or break the cake into
chunks. Place them in a glass bowl
and sprinkle with brandy. Peel,
core and slice the pears. Mix them
with the cake.

2 Pour the custard over the cake
and fruit and let set. Decorate with
whipped cream.

Serves 6–8

Tipsy Trifle

2 plain sponge cakes, 8 inches in
diameter
⅓ cup raspberry jam
12 almond-flavored cookies
2 tablespoons sliced almonds
⅔ cup sherry
2 tablespoons brandy
2 drops each lemon and orange
extract (optional)
4 egg yolks
2 teaspoons cornstarch
2 cups milk
¼ cup sugar
⅔ cup all-purpose cream
6 candied cherries
two 4-inch stems candied angelica

1 Split the sponge cakes horizontally and spread them liberally with
jam on the inside. Sandwich them
together again and cut into squares.

2 Arrange the cake squares,
cookies and almonds in the base of
a large glass bowl.

3 Measure the sherry into a pitcher
and add the brandy and fruit extracts, if wished. Pour it over the
cake and let soak.

4 In a bowl beat together the egg
yolks, cornstarch and 2 tablespoons of the milk. Meanwhile,
bring the rest of the milk to a boil in
a pan. Gradually pour the hot milk
into the bowl, beating all the time.
Pour the mixture back into the pan
and reheat, without boiling, to
thicken.

5 Pour the custard over the cakes
and leave in a cool place to set.
Whip the cream until stiff and
spread it evenly on top of the set
custard.

6 Decorate the top with a swirling
pattern and arrange the candied
cherries and 'leaves' of angelica as
decoration. Serve well chilled.

Serves 6–8

Chocolate Orange Trifle

1 chocolate jelly roll cake
2 tablespoons orange-flavored
liqueur
2 oranges
2¼ cups chocolate custard
⅔ cup all-purpose cream
6 candied cherries, halved
2 ozs. grated semisweet chocolate

1 Cut the jelly roll into slices about
¾ inch thick. Arrange them to line a
glass dish as evenly as possible.
Sprinkle them with the liqueur.

2 Grate the rind of one of the
oranges and reserve. Peel both
oranges and cut them in thin slices
across the sections, removing any
seeds. Cut the slices in half and arrange them over the slices of cake.

3 Pour the custard over the orange
and cake slices and chill to set. Beat
the cream until thick, then fold in
the grated orange rind. Decorate
the top of the trifle with whipped
cream, halved cherries and grated

chocolate. Serve cold.

Serves 6

Apple Trifle

5 cooking apples
juice and grated rind 1 lemon
½ cup sugar
squares from 2 sponge cakes
2 tablespoons sherry (optional)
⅓ cup blackberry jelly
⅔ cup all-purpose cream
8 candied cherries
two 4-inch stems candied angelica

1 Peel and core the apples and cut
them in slices. Place them with 1
tablespoon water and the lemon
juice and grated rind in a pan, cover
and cook gently for 5 minutes until
tender. Pass them through a
strainer and return the purée to the
pan with the sugar. Cook gently,
stirring frequently, until the sugar is
melted and the mixture thickened.
Cool.

2 Place a layer of sponge cake
squares on the base and sides of a
glass dish. Sprinkle with the sherry,
if used. Pour the apple purée into
the bowl and chill.

3 Melt the blackberry jelly over
low heat, stirring. Pour it over the
apple purée. Let set.

4 Beat the cream until stiff and
place it in a decorator's bag. Pipe
the cream in rosettes around the
dish where the sponge cakes meet
and in the middle. Cut the cherries
in half and the candied angelica in
diamond-shaped 'leaves,' and use
them to decorate the cream rosettes. Serve immediately or chill
until ready to serve.

Serves 8

---

*Apple Trifle contains a lovely
mixture of apple, sponge cake and
blackberry jelly, and it is topped
with cream and fruits*

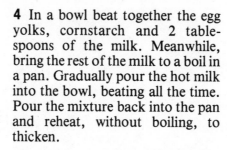

Sponge Cake Desserts

The following delicious sponge cakes filled with flavored creams, soaked in sweet syrups and often covered with exotic fresh fruits, are rich and luxurious. They make impressive desserts for special occasions and are well worth the small extra effort involved in preparing them.

Peach Chantilly

butter
2 large eggs
$\frac{1}{4}$ cup sugar
$\frac{1}{2}$ cup flour, sifted
4 large ripe peaches
$\frac{1}{3}$ cup sugar
2 tablespoons orange-flavored liqueur
1$\frac{1}{4}$ cups heavy cream, whipped
$\frac{3}{4}$ cup strained apricot jam
1 teaspoon cornstarch
$\frac{1}{2}$ cup sliced almonds

1 The day before serving, make the cake. Preheat the oven to 375°F. Butter an oblong cake pan and line its base with wax paper.

2 Place the eggs and sugar in a bowl over a saucepan of hot water. Beat until the mixture is pale and thick. Remove the bowl from the heat and continue to beat until the mixture cools. Fold in the flour and pour the cake mixture into the pan. Bake in the oven for 25 minutes and turn the cake out onto a rack to cool overnight.

3 The following day, cut the cake lengthwise into 3 layers. Bring water to a boil and scald the peaches in it for 30 seconds. Drain them and peel off their skins. Halve them and remove their pits.

Peach Chantilly is sandwiched together with layers of fresh peaches, orange liqueur, and stiffly whipped cream

4 Preheat the oven to 375°F. Place the peach halves in a shallow ovenproof dish with $\frac{3}{4}$ cup water, the sugar and liqueur. Cover and bake in the oven for 20 minutes. Allow the peaches to cool in their syrup.

5 Place $\frac{2}{3}$ of the cream in a bowl and the rest in a decorator's bag fitted with a star nozzle. Chill the bag of cream in the refrigerator.

6 Drain the peach halves, straining the syrup into a saucepan. Cut 3 peach halves into thin slices. Blend the slices with the cream in the bowl.

7 Build up the cake in the following way. Spread the bottom and middle layers of the cake with $\frac{1}{3}$ of the apricot jam and half the cream and sliced peach mixture. Sandwich them together and finish with the third piece of cake. Arrange the remaining peach halves along the top of the cake.

8 Heat the syrup, stirring in the remaining apricot jam and 2 tablespoons water. Blend the cornstarch with 1 tablespoon water and stir it into the syrup. Boil for 3 minutes.

9 Using a spoon, coat the peaches and cake with the syrup. Press the almonds to the sides of the cake with your hand and pipe the reserved cream along the top rim. Chill the cake for 2 hours and serve.

Serves 6–8

and baste with the remaining syrup. Decorate with the remaining cream and raspberries.

Serves 6–8

Strawberry Sponge Ring

butter for greasing
¾ cup butter
¾ cup sugar
3 eggs
1⅓ cups self-rising flour, sifted
1¼ cups heavy cream, whipped
2 tablespoons cherry-flavored liqueur
½ cup strained apricot jam
⅓ cup water
2 cups fresh strawberries, hulled

1 Preheat the oven to 325°F. Butter a 7-cup tube pan.

2 Beat together the butter and sugar until light and fluffy. Beat in the eggs, one at a time, adding 1 tablespoon of the flour with each egg. Gently fold in the rest of the flour. Turn into the mold and bake it in the oven for 1¼ hours. Cool the cake on a rack.

3 In a bowl blend the whipped cream and half the liqueur.

4 Place the apricot jam, remaining liqueur and water in a pan. Stirring continually, slowly bring to boil. Brush the cooled cake with the hot syrup.

5 Place the cake on a serving dish. Pile the whipped cream into the center and decorate it with half the strawberries. Arrange the rest around the dish and serve.

Serves 6–8

Tipsy Cake

2 eggs
2 egg yolks
1 cup + 3 tablespoons sugar
2 egg whites
grated rind 1 lemon
¾ cup all-purpose flour
3 tablespoons cornstarch
pinch salt
1 cup sweet white wine
1 tablespoon brandy
1¼ cups heavy cream, whipped
1¾ cups raspberries

1 Line the base of a greased 8-inch cake pan with wax paper. Preheat the oven to 350°F.

2 Place the eggs, egg yolks and 1 cup of the sugar in a bowl over a pan of hot water. Beat the mixture until it is thick. Beat the egg whites until stiff and fold them into the egg mixture with the lemon rind.

Strawberry Sponge Ring looks exotic, but is really a simple combination of a sponge cake, cream and juicy strawberries

3 Sift together the flour, cornstarch and salt and fold into the mixture. Pour it into the pan and bake in the oven for ¾–1 hour. Turn the cake onto a rack to cool.

4 Boil the remaining sugar with ¼ cup of water for 1 minute, stirring constantly. Let the syrup cool and add the wine and brandy.

5 When the cake has cooled, cut around the top, using a serrated knife to remove a cone-shaped piece 2 inches deep. Soak the cake with ⅔ of the wine syrup. Fill the cavity with half the cream and half the raspberries. Replace the cone

Look 'n Cook Chantilly Cream

1 and **2** Measure ¼ cup of the cream and the same quantity of milk into a bowl. Blend well **3** Add the rest of the cream and whisk it gently, using a circular movement from the wrist, until it begins to thicken **4** and **5** Add the sugar all at once and then the vanilla extract **6** Rapidly whisk the cream until it is very firm and forms peaks **7, 8** and **9** Decorate the Yellow Plum Cake: spoon half of the cream onto the bottom

layer of the cake and spread it evenly with a knife. Arrange the prepared plums on the bed of cream and sandwich them with the top cake layer. Fill a decorator's bag, fitted with a star nozzle, with the remaining cream. Decorate the top of the cake with swirls of cream **10** and **11** Decorate with a candied cherry and 4 pieces of angelica

Yellow Plum Cake

  ★

5 eggs, separated
grated rind 1 lemon
1¼ cups sugar
½ cup flour
½ cup cornstarch
1½ lbs. yellow plums
¼ cup butter
¼ cup brandy
4 small pieces angelica
1 candied cherry

For the Cream Chantilly:
1¼ cups heavy cream
¼ cup milk
⅞ cup confectioners' sugar
few drops vanilla extract

1 The day before serving, prepare the sponge cake. Preheat the oven to 325°F. Line the bottom of a well-greased 8-inch fluted cake pan with wax paper.

2 Beat together the egg yolks, lemon rind and 1 cup of the sugar until you have a light fluffy cream. Beat the egg whites until they stand in stiff peaks. Fold the flour, cornstarch and then the egg whites into the yolk mixture. Turn it into the pan and bake in the oven for 20 minutes. Cool the cake on a rack and then place it in the refrigerator to chill overnight.

3 Halve the plums and remove their pits. Melt the butter in a pan and add the plums. Gently sauté them, shaking the pan frequently until they turn golden. Sprinkle with the remaining sugar and cook until it begins to caramelize. Stir in the brandy. Remove the pan from the heat and let the plums cool in their syrup. Drain the plums, reserving the syrup and place them on a plate in the refrigerator.

4 Cut the cake into 2 layers and place the bottom layer on a serving dish. Generously sprinkle the bottom layer with the syrup and let it soak in.

5 Prepare the chantilly cream: measure ¼ cup of the cream into a bowl. Add the same volume of milk and blend together. Add the rest of the cream and whisk it gently with a wire whisk, using a circular movement from the wrist, until it begins to thicken. Add the sugar all at once and the vanilla. Continue to whisk the cream until it is smooth and forms firm peaks.

6 Place half the cream on the bottom layer of the cake and spread it evenly with a knife. Cover the cream with a layer of plums and sandwich the filling with the remaining layer of cake.

7 Fill a decorator's bag with the remaining cream. Pipe swirls of the cream over the top of the cake so that it is well covered. Garnish with a few pieces of angelica and a candied cherry. Serve well chilled.

Serves 8

Tip: Yellow plums may be difficult to find, and, if so, greengage plums can be used instead.

Italian Coffee Cake

 ★

flour for dusting
3 eggs
½ cup sugar
few drops almond extract
¾ cup all-purpose flour
⅔ cup heavy cream, whipped
15 coffee beans to decorate

For the Confectioners' Custard:
2 egg yolks
¼ cup sugar
2 tablespoons flour
2 tablespoons cornstarch
1¼ cups milk
1 egg white
2 teaspoons instant coffee dissolved in 4 teaspoons hot water

1 Dust 2 buttered 8-inch pans with a little flour. Preheat the oven to 375°F.

2 Place the eggs, sugar and almond extract in a bowl over a saucepan of hot water and beat until thick and creamy. Remove from the heat and continue to beat until they cool. Sift half the flour over the mixture and fold it in very gently, using a metal spoon. Blend in the remaining flour in the same way.

3 Pour the mixture into the pans, tilting them backward and forward until the mixture is spread evenly. Bake the cakes in the oven for 20-25 minutes and turn them out to cool on a rack.

4 While the cakes cool, prepare the confectioners' custard. Cream the egg yolks and sugar until thick and pale. Beat in the flour, cornstarch and ¼ cup of the milk to make a smooth paste.

5 Heat the rest of the milk in a saucepan until almost boiling and, stirring continually, pour it over the egg mixture. Return the mixture to the saucepan and stir over low heat until it boils. Remove the custard mixture from the heat.

6 Beat the egg white until stiff and fold it with the coffee into the custard. Return the custard to the pan and cook it, stirring continually, for a further 2-3 minutes. Cool.

7 Trim the minimum amount from the sponge layers to give 2 hexagons of equal size. Slice each hexagon of cake in half to give 4 layers of cake altogether.

8 Sandwich the layers of cake with the cooled confectioners' custard. Pipe the whipped cream over the top and garnish with the coffee beans.

Serves 6

Italian Coffee Cake, a real extravaganza, has sponge cake layers and confectioners' custard topped with fresh coffee beans

Raspberry Torte

¾ cup butter
¾ cup sugar
3 eggs
1½ cups self-rising flour, sifted
finely grated rind 1 orange

For the Filling and Topping:
3 tablespoons cornstarch
3 tablespoons sugar
1¼ cups milk
1¼ cups heavy cream
2 tablespoons orange-flavored
 liqueur
3 cups raspberries

1 Preheat the oven to 375°F.

2 Cream the butter and sugar together until light and fluffy, then beat in the eggs, one at a time, adding a spoonful of the flour with each to prevent curdling. Fold in the orange rind and remaining flour.

3 Divide the mixture between two buttered and lined 8-inch pans. Bake for 25-30 minutes until well-risen and firm to the touch. Turn out and cool on a wire rack.

4 Prepare the filling: blend the cornstarch and sugar to a smooth paste with a little of the milk. Heat the remaining milk and pour into the cornstarch, stirring well. Return to the pan, bring to a boil and simmer for 3 minutes, stirring continuously. Place a piece of wax paper on the custard. Cool completely.

5 Whip the cream until thick. Remove the paper from the cold custard and fold in 3 tablespoons of the cream. Fold half of the liqueur and half of the raspberries into the custard. Fold the remaining liqueur into the cream.

6 Split the cold sponge cakes in half and sandwich them together with the custard mixture, so that there are four layers of sponge and three of filling. Transfer to a serving plate.

7 Spread the cream over the top of the cake, making a thick border, 1½ inches wide, around the edge. Fill the center with the remaining raspberries.

Serves 8

Raspberry Torte is a treat for anyone with a sweet tooth. Its layers of soft sponge cake are interspersed with cream and fruit

Fruity Layer Cake

ingredients for sponge cake as in
 Raspberry Torte
1¼ cups heavy cream, whipped
confectioners' sugar
1 tablespoon rum
3 tablespoons lemon custard
1 lb. assorted canned fruit,
 drained

1 Prepare and cook the sponge cake following the instructions for the Raspberry Torte.

2 Sweeten the cream to taste with confectioners' sugar and add the rum.

3 Split the cold sponge cakes in half and spread 3 with lemon custard. Sandwich and decorate with the cream and fruit.

Serves 8

Fruity Layer Cake looks exotic, but is simple and economical to prepare using canned fruit and cream

Coffee Rum Cake

¾ cup butter
¾ cup sugar
3 eggs
1½ cups self-rising flour
¼ cup sugar
1¼ cups hot, strong coffee
2 tablespoons rum
1¼ cups heavy cream
few drops vanilla extract
2 tablespoons toasted sliced
  almonds

1 Preheat the oven to 375°F.

2 Cream the butter and sugar together until light and fluffy. Beat in the eggs, one at a time, adding a spoonful of the flour with each to prevent curdling. Sift the remaining flour and fold it into the mixture with a metal spoon.

3 Turn the mixture into a tube pan. Bake for 25-30 minutes, until well risen and firm to the touch. Turn out and cool on a wire rack.

4 Dissolve the sugar in the hot coffee, add the rum and cool.

5 When the cake is cold, return it to the clean pan and pour on the coffee. Let stand until all the liquid is absorbed, then turn onto a serving plate.

6 Whip the cream with the vanilla until it is just thick. Cover the cake completely with the cream and sprinkle with the toasted almonds to decorate. Serve chilled.

Serves 6–8

Apricot-Almond Cake is not difficult to make. It is decorated with almond-flavored cookies and then topped with canned apricots

Pear and Chocolate Sponge Cake

¾ cup butter
¾ cup sugar
3 eggs
1½ cups self-rising flour
¼ cup chopped walnuts
6 poached pear halves, drained
7 walnut halves

For the Chocolate Buttercream:
1⅔ cups confectioners' sugar
½ lb. butter
4 teaspoons cocoa
few drops vanilla extract

1 Preheat the oven to 375°F.

2 Cream the butter and sugar until light and fluffy, then beat in the eggs, one at a time, adding a spoonful of the flour with each. Sift the

remaining flour and fold in with a metal spoon.

3 Divide the mixture between two buttered and lined 8-inch pans. Bake for 25-30 minutes. Turn out and cool on a wire rack.

4 Make the chocolate buttercream: sift the confectioners' sugar and cream it with the butter until light and fluffy. Blend the cocoa with a little boiling water, and stir into the butter and sugar with a few drops of vanilla.

5 Split each sponge in half. Spread 3 of them with $\frac{1}{2}$ of the buttercream. Sandwich together with the plain sponge on top.

6 Spread the top and sides of the cake with buttercream. Press the chopped nuts onto the sides. Arrange the pears over the top and decorate with swirls of buttercream and the walnut halves.

Serves 8

Pear and Chocolate Sponge is a delicious cake which you could serve either as a dessert or for a special afternoon tea

---

Apricot-Almond Cake

$\frac{3}{4}$ **cup butter**
$\frac{3}{4}$ **cup sugar**
3 eggs
1$\frac{1}{2}$ cups self-rising flour
$\frac{1}{2}$ cup ground almonds
almond-flavored cookies
1 lb. canned apricot halves, drained
2 tablespoons apricot jam

For the Almond Filling:
2$\frac{1}{2}$ cups confectioners' sugar
$\frac{3}{4}$ cup butter
2 tablespoons milk
few drops almond extract

1 Preheat the oven to 375°F. Cream the butter and sugar until light, then beat in the eggs, one at a time, adding a spoonful of the flour with each. Add the almonds, then

sift the remaining flour and fold in with a metal spoon.

2 Divide the mixture between two buttered and lined 8-inch pans. Bake for 25-30 minutes. Turn out and cool.

3 Make the almond filling: cream the confectioners' sugar with the butter until light and fluffy. Beat in the milk and almond extract.

4 Sandwich the cold sponge cakes with half the almond filling, and spread the rest over the top and sides.

5 Press crushed cookies into the sides of the cake. Drain the apricot halves, reserving 2 tablespoons of the syrup and arrange the apricot halves, cut side down, over the top of the cake. Melt the jam with the reserved apricot syrup and use to brush over the apricots.

Serves 8

Apple and Hazelnut Cake

¼ lb. butter
½ cup sugar
2 eggs, separated
½ cup ground hazelnuts, toasted
1 cup + 2 tablespoons self-rising flour
pinch salt
1 tablespoon milk

For the Filling:
3 tart apples
2 tablespoons apricot jam
juice and grated rind 1 lemon
3 tablespoons sugar
3 tablespoons brandy
1¼ cups heavy cream

1 Preheat the oven to 375°F. Cream the butter and sugar until light and beat in the egg yolks. Stir in ¾ of the hazelnuts. Fold in the flour and salt with the milk. Beat the egg whites until stiff and fold in with a metal spoon.

2 Turn the mixture into a buttered and floured 8-inch cake pan, and bake for 25 minutes, until the cake has shrunk slightly from the sides of the pan and is firm. Cool on a wire rack.

3 Peel, core and slice the apples, and place in a small pan with the jam, lemon rind and juice. Cover and cook gently until the apples are soft. Cool.

4 Dissolve the sugar in a small pan with 3 tablespoons water, bring to a boil and boil until syrupy. Stir in 2 tablespoons of the brandy and cool.

5 Whip the cream until thick and fold in the remaining brandy.

6 Split the cold cake and sprinkle each half with some of the syrup. Sandwich the sponges with some of the cream and the apples. Moisten the cake with the remaining syrup.

7 Decorate with the remaining cream and reserved hazelnuts.

Serves 6–8

Strawberry Cream Cake

¾ cup flour
½ teaspoon cinnamon
pinch salt
3 eggs
½ cup sugar
finely grated rind ½ lemon
1¼ cups heavy cream
few drops vanilla extract
1 pint strawberries, hulled
6 macaroons, crushed
½ cup red currant jelly
1 tablespoon orange juice

1 Preheat the oven to 350°F. Sift the flour with the cinnamon and salt.

2 Break the eggs into a bowl and gradually beat in the sugar. Stand the bowl over a pan of hot water and beat until thick and pale in color. Remove from the heat and continue to beat until cool.

3 Fold in the flour and the grated lemon rind. Pour the mixture into a buttered and lined 8-inch cake pan. Bake in the preheated oven for 15-20 minutes. Turn out and cool on a wire rack.

4 Whip the cream with a few drops of vanilla and divide between two bowls. Slice one-quarter of the strawberries and mix with one bowl of the cream. Use to sandwich the sponge cakes together.

5 Use the remaining cream to pipe a decorative border around the top of the cake and to spread around the sides. Press the crushed macaroons onto the sides.

6 Heat the red currant jelly with the orange juice until completely dissolved. Allow to cool, without setting. Arrange the remaining strawberries over the top of the cake inside the cream border, and brush with the red currant glaze.

Serves 8

Chocolate Rum Cake

1¼ cups flour
¼ cup cocoa
½ teaspoon salt
½ teaspoon baking powder
⅔ cup soft brown sugar
2 eggs, separated
⅓ cup oil
⅓ cup milk
½ teaspoon vanilla extract
¼ cup rum
⅔ cup light cream
⅔ cup heavy cream
3-4 ozs. grated semisweet chocolate

1 Preheat the oven to 350°F.

2 Sift together the flour, cocoa powder, salt and baking powder and stir in the sugar.

3 Mix together the egg yolks, oil, milk and vanilla and beat with the flour mixture to a smooth batter.

4 Beat the egg whites until stiff and peaking and fold into the batter with a metal spoon.

5 Divide the mixture between two 8-inch buttered and lined pans and bake for about 30 minutes until well-risen and firm to the touch. Turn out and cool on a wire rack.

6 Return the cold cakes to the clean pans and sprinkle with the rum. Let stand until all the rum has been absorbed.

7 Whip the creams together until thick. Use a little less than half to sandwich the sponge cakes together, then transfer the cake to a serving plate. Spread the remaining cream over the top and sides. Press the chocolate onto the sides and sprinkle over the top.

Serves 8

Strawberry Cream Cake and Chocolate Rum Cake are two quite different treats which cannot fail to impress

Meringue Desserts

Meringue desserts are always popular and, although they look impressive, they are really very easy to make. There are three different types of meringue:

Swiss Meringue is the one that most people know about and is used for meringue shells and the topping on most hot meringue puddings.

American Meringue is another topping for meringue pies, but cream of tartar and vinegar are added to the meringue mixture.

Cooked Meringue is made with confectioners' sugar and is hard and powdery. It is suitable for cakes or as a topping for desserts.

Most of our recipes are made with the Swiss meringue mixture. A wire whisk is best if you are to obtain a stiff, shiny meringue — electric and rotary beaters can be used with some success but the results will not be as good. However, they do save you time and arm-ache!

Strawberry Meringue Tart

3 egg whites
¾ cup sugar
1⅓ cups strawberries
1¼ cups heavy cream
2 tablespoons orange-flavored
   liqueur

1 Preheat the oven to 250°F. or even lower, if possible.

2 Cover a baking sheet with some wax paper. Draw a circle of 8 inches in diameter on the paper.

3 Beat the egg whites until stiff, then beat in half of the sugar. When stiff, fold in the remaining sugar with a metal spoon.

4 Spread some of the meringue over the circle to make the base of the tart. Fill a decorator's bag, fitted with a large star nozzle, with the rest of the meringue and pipe large, attractive rosettes around the base to form the sides of the tart. Bake in the oven until dry and white (about 1½–2 hours). Do not allow the meringue to brown. Cool the meringue shell on a wire rack.

5 Hull and wash the strawberries. Whip the cream until stiff and stir in the liqueur.

6 Place a layer of cream inside the base of the meringue and pile the strawberries on top. Place the rest of the cream in a bowl and serve separately.

Serves 4–6

Tips: You can fill this meringue shell with any fresh fruit. Peaches, raspberries and bananas are all suitable. To make it more attractive, you can pipe rosettes of cream across the top and around the sides of the meringue shell. Another idea is to soak the fruit in brandy or a liqueur before filling the shell. Be careful to drain them thoroughly, though, as the liqueur will make the meringue soggy.

If you prefer, you can make individual meringue shells so that your guests can have one each. This is a good idea for parties and buffets. Just draw smaller circles on the wax paper and pipe the meringue as before.

Flamed Pineapple Meringue

2 whole eggs
6 egg yolks
¾ cup confectioners' sugar
1 cup + 2 tablespoons flour,
   sifted
1 cup pineapple juice
3 cups milk
1 teaspoon vanilla extract
10 pineapple slices
¼ cup butter, softened
⅔ cup white rum

For the Meringue:
4 egg whites
¾ cup confectioners' sugar

1 In a mixing bowl, blend together the whole eggs, egg yolks and confectioners' sugar. Beat well, then mix in the flour. Stir in the pineapple juice.

2 Heat the milk in a heavy saucepan and, when boiling, pour it over the egg and pineapple mixture, stirring all the time. Add the vanilla and pour back into the saucepan.

3 Return the pan to the heat and boil for several minutes, stirring continuously, until it thickens. Then remove from the heat.

4 Cut 2 of the pineapple slices into cubes and mix into the pastry cream. Then stir in the butter and ¼ cup of the rum.

5 Preheat the oven to 400°F.

6 Beat the egg whites until stiff. Gradually add the sugar, beating all the time until stiff and shiny.

7 Spread the pastry cream over the base of an ovenproof dish. Arrange the remaining pineapple slices on top and then cover with the meringue. Place in the oven and bake until the meringue is cooked and golden.

8 Just before serving, heat the rest of the rum in a small saucepan. Pour it over the meringue, ignite it, and serve the flaming dish to your guests.

Serves 8

Tip: There are a number of variations on this dish which you can try. You can substitute brandy or another spirit for rum and can even use alternative fruits for the filling.

Strawberry Meringue is filled with delicious orange liqueur-flavored cream and then topped with juicy strawberries

Quick Vacherin

$\frac{2}{3}$ cup heavy cream
few drops vanilla extract
1 meringue shell
12-16 scoops ice cream (raspberry
  or strawberry)
$2\frac{2}{3}$ cups strawberries, hulled
8 pink oval-shaped meringues
  (see Cream Meringues)
8 brown oval-shaped meringues
  (see Cream Meringues)

1 Whip the cream until thick and stir in the vanilla. Transfer to a decorator's bag fitted with a large star nozzle.

2 Place the meringue base on a serving plate and cover with the ice cream. Pile the strawberries on top, reserving a few for decoration.

3 Stand the pink and brown meringues alternately around the sides, pressing onto the ice cream to secure.

4 Pipe the cream in swirls around the meringues and over the strawberries, and decorate with the reserved strawberries. Serve immediately.

Serves 6–8

Coconut Pyramids

lard for greasing
2 egg whites
$\frac{2}{3}$ cup sugar
$1\frac{1}{2}$ cups shredded coconut

1 Preheat the oven to 275°F. Grease a baking sheet and cover with wax paper.

2 Beat the egg whites until they are stiff and peaking, and fold in the sugar and coconut with a metal spoon.

3 Put the mixture onto the prepared baking sheet in 12 small pyramids and press into a neat shape. Bake in the oven for $\frac{3}{4}$–1 hour until the pyramids are very

lightly browned. Cool on a wire rack.

Makes 12

Cherry Alaska Tarts

$\frac{3}{4}$ cup butter cookie crumbs
3 tablespoons sugar
1 teaspoon ground ginger
$\frac{1}{3}$ cup butter

For the Filling:
2 egg whites
$\frac{1}{3}$ cup sugar
12 ozs. canned cherries, drained
1 tablespoon finely chopped
  preserved gingerroot in syrup
1 tablespoon ginger syrup
6 scoops vanilla ice cream

1 Preheat the oven to 350°F.

2 Crush the cookies finely and stir in the sugar and ground ginger. Melt the butter and mix well with the crumbs. Divide the mixture between six 4-inch fluted flan pans, and, using the back of a teaspoon, press the mixture firmly and evenly over the base and sides.

3 Bake in the preheated oven for 10 minutes. Allow to cool in the pans.

4 Increase the oven temperature to 450°F. Remove the cool cookie crusts from the pans and place on a baking sheet.

5 Make the filling: beat the egg whites until they are softly peaking, add half the sugar and continue to beat until glossy and firm. Gently fold in the remaining sugar with a metal spoon.

6 Divide the cherries among the crusts and sprinkle with the finely chopped gingerroot and the syrup. Put a scoop of ice cream on top and cover the ice cream and fruit com-

pletely with the meringue. Put into the oven for 2-3 minutes until the outside of the meringue begins to brown.

7 Slide each Alaska Tart onto an individual serving plate and serve immediately.

Serves 6

Cream Meringues

2 egg whites
$\frac{1}{2}$ cup sugar
$\frac{2}{3}$ cup heavy cream
optional: a few drops of food
  coloring of choice

1 Preheat the oven to 225°F. Line a baking sheet with aluminum foil or wax paper.

2 Beat the egg whites until they are softly peaking, add half the sugar and continue to beat until the mixture is glossy and firm. Fold in the remaining sugar with a metal spoon.

3 Transfer the mixture to a decorator's bag fitted with a large star nozzle, and pipe 10-12 swirls onto the prepared baking sheet. Alternatively, you can spoon the mixture in neat mounds.

4 Dry the meringues in the coolest part of the oven for 2-3 hours, until the meringues are firm and crisp, but still white. If the meringues begin to brown, prop open the oven door a little.

5 Remove the meringues from the paper and cool on a wire rack.

6 Whip the cream until it is just thick and use to sandwich the meringue shells in pairs.

Makes 5 or 6

Quick Vacherin is as easy to make as its name suggests, since it uses meringues and ice cream with strawberries

Black Currant Meringue Pie

1 cup + 2 tablespoons flour
pinch salt
1 teaspoon cinnamon
$\frac{1}{4}$ cup softened butter
$\frac{1}{4}$ cup sugar
2 eggs, separated
$\frac{1}{2}$ teaspoon vanilla extract
12 ozs. canned black currants
1 teaspoon cornstarch
3 tablespoons sugar

For the Topping:
$\frac{1}{2}$ cup sugar
$\frac{1}{2}$ teaspoon cinnamon

1 Sift the flour, salt and cinnamon onto the table. Make a well in the center and in this, place the butter, sugar, egg yolks and vanilla.

2 With the fingertips of one hand, blend together the butter, sugar and egg yolks until well mixed, then work in the flour. Knead lightly until smooth, then wrap and chill for about 1 hour.

3 Meanwhile, make the filling. Pour off half the juice from the black currants, using a little to blend with the cornstarch. Place the remaining black currants and juice in a pan with the sugar and bring to a boil. Add the blended cornstarch and simmer for 3 minutes, stirring continuously. Cool.

4 Preheat the oven to 375°F. Roll out the pastry and use to line a 7-inch flan ring, set on a baking sheet. Line with wax paper, fill with baking beans and bake in the pre-heated oven for 15 minutes. Remove the paper and beans and bake for a further 5 minutes, or until a pale brown. Cool in the flan ring.

5 Reduce the oven temperature to 300°F. Pour the black currant mixture into the pie shell.

6 Make the topping: beat the egg whites until stiff and peaking. Add 2 teaspoons of the sugar and beat until firm, then fold in the remaining sugar and the cinnamon with a metal spoon. Spoon the meringue on top of the pie to completely cover the filling and bake in the oven for 30 minutes.

7 Serve warm or cold.

Serves 5 or 6

Tip: If black currants are not available, you can replace them with the same weight of pitted black cherries, blackberries or damson plums.

Swiss Peach Meringue, topped with meringue pyramids, has a jelly roll base with peaches, custard and macaroons

Swiss Peach Meringue

1 jelly roll
4 almond macaroons, crushed
2 tablespoons brandy
2 peaches, pitted, skinned and sliced
3 tablespoons custard mix
$2\frac{1}{2}$ tablespoons sugar
$1\frac{3}{4}$ cups milk

For the Topping:
2 egg whites
$\frac{1}{2}$ cup sugar
1 tablespoon sliced almonds

1 Slice the jelly roll and arrange the slices around the sides and base of an overproof serving bowl.

Sprinkle on the macaroons, then moisten with the brandy. Arrange the sliced peaches over the top.

2 Make the custard: blend the custard mix and sugar with a little of the milk. Bring the rest of the milk to a boil and pour onto the custard mixture, stirring. Return to the pan and simmer for 3 minutes, stirring. Cool slightly, then pour gently over the peaches and sponge cake.

3 Beat the egg whites until they are stiff and peaking. Add 2 teaspoons of the sugar and beat until firm. Carefully fold in the remaining sugar with a metal spoon. Transfer the mixture to a decorator's bag fitted with a star-shaped nozzle and cover the custard with peaks of meringue.

4 Stud some of the peaks with the flaked almonds and place under the

Creole Meringue Cake has all the color and exciting flavors of South America and the French Caribbean, where it originated

broiler until golden brown. Serve immediately.

Serves 4 or 5

Créole Meringue Cake

1 cup sugar
4 eggs, separated
¼ cup flour
7½ tablespoons cornstarch
pinch salt
½ cup candied cherries
½ cup cherry-flavored liqueur

¼ cup rum

For the Meringue Topping:
2 egg whites
pinch salt
2 tablespoons confectioners' sugar

1 Preheat the oven to 350°F.

2 Add half of the sugar to the egg yolks and beat together until light and fluffy. Sift the flours together and fold into the egg yolk mixture with a metal spoon.

3 Beat the egg whites and salt in a separate bowl until they are stiff and peaking. Add the remaining sugar, a little at a time, beating well after each addition.

4 Carefully fold the egg whites into the yolk mixture and pour into an 8-inch buttered and floured cake pan. Bake in the preheated oven for 20 minutes. Increase the oven temperature to 375°F., and bake for a further 10 minutes. Do not turn off the oven since it will be needed at a later stage. Turn out the cooked cake onto a cooling rack and cool completely.

5 Cut the cherries into small pieces and place them in a bowl with the liqueur and rum for 15 minutes. When the cake is cold, slice it in half through the middle and sandwich together again with the cherries and their liquid. Place on a flat ovenproof serving dish.

6 Prepare the meringue topping: beat the egg whites with the salt and sugar until thick and firm. Spread the mixture evenly over the top and sides of the cake, and bake in the hot oven for 8-10 minutes until golden brown.

7 Cool the cake completely before serving.

Serves 6

Tip: For a crisper, crunchier topping, sprinkle some crushed toasted peanuts over the meringue before baking. The filling can also be altered — try using cubed pineapple or papaya instead of the cherries.

Dacquoise

Dacquoise is a meringue to which ground almonds or hazelnuts have been added. The following recipes are all for cakes based on this delicious meringue and filled with nut or liqueur-flavored creams. Rich and sweet, these extravagant and attractive cakes make impressive desserts for a special occasion.

Success Cake

1½ cups ground hazelnuts
1⅓ cups sugar
8 egg whites
½ teaspoon vanilla extract
2 tablespoons orange-flavored liqueur
1¼ cups heavy cream, whipped
⅓ cup apricot jam, strained
¾ cup confectioners' sugar

1 Preheat the oven to 375°F.

2 Reserve 2 tablespoons of the ground hazelnuts and mix the rest with the sugar. In another bowl beat the egg whites with the vanilla until they are stiff. Fold the egg whites into the hazelnut mixture and, following the instructions given in Almond Meringue Cake, pipe three 9-inch circles onto a lightly floured metal tray. Bake in the oven for 20-25 minutes. Cool on the tray.

3 Stir half of the liqueur into the whipped cream. Slide one layer of meringue onto a serving dish. Spread with half of the cream. Cover with another layer of meringue, then the remaining cream and finish with the final layer of meringue.

4 Heat the apricot jam in a saucepan and spread it evenly over the top of the cake. In another sauce-pan combine the remaining liqueur, the confectioners' sugar and the reserved hazelnuts with 1 tablespoon water. Slowly bring these ingredients to a boil, stirring continually. Remove from the heat and, when the glaze begins to cool, spread it over the entire cake. Allow the glaze to set and chill the cake in the refrigerator before serving.

Serves 8

Almond Meringue Cake

8 egg whites
pinch salt
1⅓ cups sugar
1¼ cups ground blanched almonds
3 tablespoons cornstarch
2 tablespoons flour
¾ cup heavy cream, whipped
⅓ cup sliced almonds

For the Chocolate Cream:
½ cup sugar
¼ cup chopped almonds
2 ozs. dark chocolate
½ lb. unsalted butter, softened
⅔ cup confectioners' sugar

1 In a bowl, beat the egg whites with a pinch of salt until they are white and fluffy. Add half of the sugar, a tablespoon at a time, and continue to beat until the mixture forms stiff peaks.

2 In another bowl, blend together the ground almonds, remaining sugar and cornstarch. Gently blend half of the egg white mixture with the almond mixture and then fold in the remaining half.

3 Preheat the oven to 350°F. Sprinkle a large baking sheet with the flour. Using a 9-inch plate as an outline, draw 3 circles on the tray with a fine brush. Fill a decorator's bag fitted with a ½-inch nozzle with the meringue mixture. Starting at the center of each circle pipe outward in circles until each one has been completely covered with a ½ inch thick layer of meringue. Bake them on the middle shelf of the oven for 20-25 minutes. Remove and cool on the tray.

4 Prepare the chocolate cream. Place the sugar in a saucepan with 1 tablespoon water. Cook gently until they caramelize and turn golden brown. Stir in the chopped almonds and pour the praline onto a well-buttered metal tray. Allow the praline to harden and then crush it to a powder with a rolling pin.

5 Melt the chocolate and stir it into the crushed praline. In a bowl, beat together the soft butter and confectioners' sugar until soft and fluffy. Mix this soft butter mixture with the chocolate and praline until you have a cream of even consistency.

6 Very gently slide a meringue layer onto a serving dish — be careful not to break it.

7 Place ¾ of the chocolate cream in a decorator's bag and, starting at the outer rim pipe circles of the cream over the meringue at 1-inch intervals until you reach the center. Dip a spatula in hot water and use it to spread the cream more evenly. Cover with another layer of meringue. Spread ¾ of the whipped cream over this layer and top with the remaining meringue layer.

8 Carefully pipe the remaining chocolate cream over the top and spread it evenly with a heated knife. Sprinkle the top with the flaked almonds and pipe rosettes of the remaining whipped cream around the rim and in the center. Chill for 1 hour in the refrigerator and serve.

Serves 8

Almond Meringue Cake has a sophisticated look which may take some care to achieve but is well worth the extra effort

Dacquoise Sévillane

8 egg whites
pinch salt
$\frac{7}{8}$ cup sugar
$\frac{1}{2}$ cup blanched hazelnuts
$\frac{3}{4}$ cup ground blanched almonds
grated rind 1 small orange
1 tablespoon butter

For the Filling:
$\frac{1}{2}$ cup preserved orange peel
1 cup milk
4 egg yolks
$\frac{1}{2}$ cup sugar
$\frac{7}{8}$ cup butter
$\frac{1}{4}$ cup orange-flavored liqueur
$\frac{1}{3}$ cup toasted sliced almonds

1 Preheat the oven to 325°F. Place the egg whites in a bowl and add a pinch of salt. Beat them and when they start to get fluffy, add the sugar gradually. Continue to beat until stiff.

2 Put the blanched hazelnuts in a grater or coffee grinder and grind to a fine powder. Fold the ground almonds, ground hazelnuts and grated orange rind into the beaten egg whites.

3 Butter three 8-inch flan rings and place them on a baking sheet. Spread the egg white mixture in the three molds. Place in the oven and bake for about 30 minutes until crisp.

4 Meanwhile, finely chop half the preserved orange peel, keeping the other half for garnish. Heat the milk in a saucepan.

5 Place the 4 egg yolks in a bowl and beat. Add the sugar gradually and beat until the mixture is pale and creamy. Stir in the hot milk to blend well. Put the mixture in a pan over a double boiler and cook over low heat, stirring all the time with a wooden spoon. Do not let the mixture boil. When the custard has thickened enough to coat the spoon, plunge the base of the pan in a bowl of cold water to stop the cooking. Cool.

6 Cream the butter in another bowl until light and fluffy. Add the liqueur and finely chopped orange peel. When the custard mixture is cool, beat in the butter and whip until the mixture is smooth and quite stiff.

7 Put one of the meringues on a serving dish. Spread $\frac{1}{3}$ of the cream filling on it and top with a second meringue. Cover that with another $\frac{1}{3}$ of cream and top with the third meringue. Spread the remaining cream around the sides. Cut the rest of the preserved orange peel into diamond shapes and garnish the top with them. Press toasted sliced almonds around the sides and scatter some on top. Dust with a little confectioners' sugar and serve.

Serves 6–8

Tip: This cake can be varied by changing the filling flavor and leaving the grated orange rind out of the meringue mixture. Try a coffee or lemon-flavored cream, or add finely chopped pistachio nuts to a liqueur-flavored filling.

Dacquoise Sévillane is a sophisticated dessert you can serve at special dinner parties for entertaining friends

All about Tarts, Flans and Pies

Apple Bakewell Tart

Tarts and Flans

Tarts and flans are tremendously versatile; whether rich in protein or light and fruity, from practical weekday snacks to sophisticated party desserts, there's something suitable for every occasion. Try some of the more unusual combinations — cottage cheese filling in an almond-flavored crust, rich eggnog in a chocolate-flavored shell, or even a shell of ice cream filled with creamy coffee and honey.

Whole Wheat Yogurt Flan

dough for one 8-inch pie crust
3 fresh peaches
1¼ cups plain yogurt
1⅓ cups cottage cheese
3 tablespoons honey
½ teaspoon vanilla extract

1 Preheat the oven to 400°F.

2 Roll out the dough and use it to line an 8-inch flan ring. Set on a baking sheet. Bake for 20 minutes. Cool.

3 Peel and halve the peaches, remove the pits and slice the fruit neatly.

4 Mix together the yogurt and cottage cheese and pass through a strainer. Stir in the honey and vanilla.

5 Arrange two-thirds of the sliced peaches in the cold flan shell and spoon over the yogurt mixture. Top with the remaining sliced peaches and chill in the refrigerator for several hours.

Serves 6

Crunchy Peanut Tart

dough for one 8-inch pie crust
3 eggs
¼ cup corn syrup
¼ cup butter
½ teaspoon vanilla extract
¼ lb. unsalted peanuts, chopped

1 Preheat the oven to 400°F.

2 Roll out the dough and use it to line an 8-inch flan ring set on a baking sheet. Line with paper and fill with baking beans and bake for 15 minutes. Remove the paper and beans and bake for a further 5 minutes. Remove from the oven and reduce the oven temperature to 325°F.

3 Beat the eggs and syrup together. Melt the butter and add it with the vanilla and peanuts to the egg mixture. Pour into the flan shell.

4 Bake for 30 minutes, cool slightly, then remove the flan ring. Serve warm or cold.

Serves 6

Strawberry Cream Flan

dough for one 8-inch pie crust
2 cups strawberries
⅔ cup heavy cream
⅔ cup light cream
2 tablespoons sugar
2 tablespoons strawberry jam
2 teaspoons water

1 Preheat the oven to 400°F.

2 Roll out the dough and use it to line an 8-inch flan ring, set on a baking sheet. Line with paper, fill with baking beans and bake for 15 minutes. Remove the paper and beans and bake for a further 5 minutes. Cool, then remove the flan ring.

3 Hull the strawberries and slice them. Whip the creams together and fold in the sugar and half of the strawberries. Spoon into the flan shell and decorate with the remaining sliced strawberries.

4 Melt the jam with the water, strain and brush over the strawberries to glaze. Serve chilled.

Serves 6

Tarte Tatin

dough for one 8-inch pie crust
4 tart apples
⅓ cup butter
⅔ cups sugar

1 Preheat the oven to 400°F.

2 Make the filling: peel, quarter and core the apples, then cut them into slices.

3 Grease an 8-inch flan pan with half of the butter and sprinkle with half of the sugar. Arrange the apple slices on it, then sprinkle with the remaining sugar and dot with the remaining butter.

4 Roll out the dough thinly, and cut a neat circle a little larger than the flan pan. Place the circle over the apples, tucking the edge inside the flan pan, and bake in the preheated oven for 25-30 minutes until the dough is cooked and the apples have caramelized.

5 Invert the tart onto a serving plate and serve warm.

Serves 6

Tarte Tatin is baked upside down and then inverted onto the plate to reveal its sticky, golden caramelized filling

Russian Apricot Tart

dough for one 9-inch pie crust
1 lb. fresh apricots
½ cup brown sugar
1 teaspoon mixed mace and
  allspice
beaten egg to glaze

1 Preheat the oven to 400°F.

2 Roll out two-thirds of the dough and use it to line a 9-inch flan pan. Prick the base with a fork.

3 Halve the apricots and remove the pits. Arrange them, cut-side down, in the crust, and sprinkle with the sugar and spice.

4 Roll out the remaining dough and cut into strips ½ inch wide, using a ravioli cutter. Place the strips, lattice-fashion, across the tart, sealing the ends of the strips to the tart edge with a little water.

5 Brush the strips with beaten egg to glaze, place the flan pan on a baking sheet and bake in the pre-

Russian Apricot Tart is a very attractive dessert with its lattice pattern of crinkle-cut strips of crisp pastry

heated oven for 25-30 minutes.

Serves 6

Chocolate Eggnog Flan

1¼ cups flour
3 tablespoons instant chocolate
  drink mix
¼ cup butter
3 tablespoons lard or shortening
2 tablespoons cold water

For the Filling:
6 tablespoons sugar
2 eggs
¼ cup flour
1¼ cups milk
1 teaspoon vanilla extract

⅔ cup light cream
1 tablespoon rum
grated nutmeg

1 Preheat the oven to 400°F. Sift the flour and chocolate and add the lard or shortening, cut into pieces. Rub in until the mixture resembles fine breadcrumbs. Mix to a firm dough with the water.

2 Knead the dough lightly and roll out to fit an 8-inch flan ring. Bake for 20 minutes.

3 Make the filling: place ¼ cup of the sugar in a bowl with 1 egg and 1 egg yolk. Beat well and mix in the flour. Warm the milk with the vanilla and pour onto the egg mixture, stirring. Return to the pan and stir over gentle heat until thickened. Pour into the crust, cool, then chill.

4 Beat the remaining egg white until stiff and peaking, then beat in the rest of the sugar. Whip the cream with the rum and fold gently into the egg whites. Spread the mixture over the filling and sprinkle with nutmeg.

Serves 6

Lemon Breeze Tart

⅓ **cup butter**
¾ **cup butter cookie crumbs**
3 **tablespoons sugar**
1¼ **cups canned sweetened**
  condensed milk
finely grated rind and juice 2 large
  lemons
⅔ **cup light cream**

1 Preheat the oven to 350°F.

2 Melt the butter and stir in the crushed cookies and sugar. Using the back of a metal spoon, press the mixture into the base and up the sides of an 8-inch flan ring set on a baking sheet. Bake for 10 minutes,

then cool in the ring.

3 Combine the condensed milk and lemon rind and juice and stir until the mixture thickens. Add the cream, pour into the cooled flan crust and chill for 2 hours.

Serves 6

Blueberry Surprise Tart

dough for one 9-inch pie crust

Blueberry Surprise Tart has a hidden layer of lemon custard which makes a sweet contrast to the blueberries

¼ **cup lemon custard**
4 **cups blueberries**
½ **cup sugar**
3 **tablespoons cornstarch**
beaten egg to glaze

1 Preheat the oven to 375°F.

2 Roll out two-thirds of the dough and use to line a 9-inch flan pan. Prick the base and spread with the lemon custard.

3 Fill the tart with the blueberries, sprinkling with the sugar and cornstarch.

4 Roll out the remaining dough and cut into strips ½ inch wide. Place the strips, lattice-fashion, across the tart, sealing the ends to the tart edge with water.

5 Brush the strips with beaten egg to glaze, place the flan pan on a baking sheet and bake in the oven for 30-40 minutes.

Serves 6

Mint Chocolate Flan

3 ozs. bitter chocolate
1 tablespoon butter
1⅓ cups gingersnap cookie crumbs
3 egg yolks
½ cup sugar
2 tablespoons crème de menthe
2 teaspoons unflavored gelatin
2 tablespoons water
few drops green food coloring
⅔ cup heavy cream, whipped

1 Melt the chocolate and butter in a pan and blend in the cookie crumbs. Butter an 8-inch flan pan and spread the crumb mixture evenly over the base and sides, pressing it down firmly. Chill in the refrigerator.

2 In a bowl, beat together the egg yolks, sugar and crème de menthe until smooth and thick.

3 Sprinkle the gelatin over the water in a small bowl and stand it in a pan of hot water. Stir until the gelatin has dissolved. Allow it to cool slightly and gradually beat it into the egg mixture. Fold in the food coloring and the whipped cream. When the mixture is about to set, pour it into the flan crust. Chill until set, and serve.

Serves 6

Apricot Marshmallow Tart

1 lb. fresh apricots, pitted
¾ cup sugar
2 tablespoons cornstarch
1 teaspoon each ground cinnamon and nutmeg
dough for one 8-inch pie crust
¼ lb. miniature marshmallows

1 Place the apricots in a pan with a little water and ⅔ of the sugar. Cook gently over low heat until the fruit is soft.

2 Blend the rest of the sugar, the cornstarch and the spices with a little water. Add this to the fruit and cook until the mixture thickens.

3 Roll out the dough and line a buttered 8-inch flan pan. Preheat the oven to 425°F.

4 Pour the fruit mixture into the uncooked flan. Roll out the leftover trimmings of dough and cut into ¼-inch strips. Arrange these in a lattice pattern over the top of the fruit mixture.

5 Bake the tart in the middle of the oven for 25-30 minutes. Remove it from the oven and place a marshmallow in each square of the lattice pattern. Return to the oven for 5 minutes until the marshmallow is lightly browned. Serve with cream or custard.

Serves 6

Tip: This tart can be made with a variety of other seasonal fruits.

Egg Custard Tart

dough for one 7-inch pie crust
2 eggs
2 tablespoons sugar
1¼ cups milk
1 teaspoon ground nutmeg

1 Roll out the dough on a floured board and line a 7-inch flan pan. Preheat the oven to 425°F.

2 In a bowl, beat the eggs with the sugar. Warm the milk in a pan and pour it into the egg mixture, stirring. Strain the custard into the uncooked flan shell and sprinkle the nutmeg evenly over the top.

3 Bake in the middle of the oven for 10 minutes. Reduce the oven temperature to 350°F. and cook for 20 minutes more, or until the custard is set. Cool and serve.

Serves 4–6

Tutti Frutti Tart

dough for one 8-inch pie crust
7 large strawberries
1 banana
1 sweet orange
1 peach, or 6 canned peach slices
2 ozs. canned cherries
1 lemon
⅓ cup apricot jam
1 tablespoon water

1 Preheat the oven to 425°F. Roll out the pastry ⅛ inch thick. Butter an 8-inch fluted flan pan and line it with the pastry. Bake for 20 minutes until the flan shell is crisp and golden-brown. Allow to cool.

2 Prepare the fruit: wash and hull the strawberries, peel and slice the banana. Cut the orange into thin slices and remove any seeds; cut the slices in quarters. Peel and slice the peach, if using a fresh one. Drain the canned cherries. Thinly slice the lemon and quarter the slices.

3 In a pan melt the apricot jam with the water. Pass through a strainer.

4 Arrange the fruit in the flan shell as illustrated, filling ⅙ of the flan with each fruit and finishing with a strawberry in the middle. Pour the apricot glaze over the top. Chill and serve with whipped cream.

Serves 6

Tutti Frutti Tart is a genuine Italian showpiece that is simple to make, and can be filled with a variety of fresh fruits

Apricot Cheese Flan

2¾ cups flour
pinch salt
1 teaspoon cinnamon
6 tablespoons butter
¼ cup lard or shortening
⅓ cup water
12 ozs. cream cheese
½ cup sugar
1 teaspoon grated orange rind
2 tablespoons orange juice
2 tablespoons heavy cream
2 lbs. canned apricot halves with
   syrup
2 tablespoons strained apricot jam
1 tablespoon cornstarch
1⅓ cups strawberries, hulled

1 Preheat the oven to 400°F.

2 Sift the flour with the salt and cinnamon into a bowl and rub in the butter and lard or shortening until it resembles fine breadcrumbs. Add the water and mix to a firm dough.

3 Knead the dough on a floured board until it is smooth. Roll it out to a thickness of ¼ inch and use it to line a 12 × 8 inch flan dish. Remove the trimmings and roll them into strips long enough to cover the rims of the flan dish. Brush the rims with a little water and arrange the strips on top. Flute the strips with a knife and prick the bottom with a fork, then bake the crust for 20 minutes. Cool in the dish.

4 Meanwhile, blend together the cream cheese, sugar, orange rind, juice and cream.

5 Strain the syrup from the apricots into a saucepan and drain the halved apricots on absorbent paper.

6 Gently heat the syrup and stir in the apricot jam. Mix the cornstarch with a little syrup and stir it back into the saucepan. Boil for 1-2 minutes until the syrup is clear.

Easter Baskets are filled with a creamy and smooth almond butter filling, then topped with apricot halves

---

7 Spread the cream cheese mixture over the bottom of the crust and arrange the apricot halves in rows, hollow side upward, on top. Spoon on the syrup and garnish with the strawberries. Chill and serve.

Serves 8–10

Easter Baskets

dough for one 9-inch pie crust
¼ cup butter
¼ cup sugar
1 egg
2 tablespoons flour
⅓ cup ground almonds
12 canned apricot halves, well
   drained
⅔ cup heavy cream, whipped
12 angelica strips

1 Roll out the dough on a lightly floured board. Using a 2½-inch fluted cutter, stamp out 12 rounds. Place the rounds in 12 tartlet pans.

2 Cream the butter and sugar together and beat in the egg. Blend in the flour and ground almonds and divide the mixture between the 12 pastry shells. Bake them in the oven for 20 minutes. Remove and allow them to cool.

3 Place an apricot half on top of each tartlet. Fill a decorator's bag, fitted with a small star nozzle, with the cream. Pipe rosettes of cream around each apricot. Bend each stick of angelica to form the shape of a handle and insert in the tartlets.

Makes 12 tartlets

Apricot Cheese Flan: a colorful combination of canned apricots and strawberries conceals a layer of cream cheese

Raspberry Rumba

one 10-inch sponge cake shell
⅓ cup raspberry jam
3 cups fresh raspberries
2 tablespoons cherry-flavored
  liqueur
⅓ cup all-purpose cream

1 Place the sponge cake on a serving dish. Spread the raspberry jam over the base.

2 Clean the raspberries and remove any crushed or discolored ones. Arrange the rest of them on the cake, from the outer edge toward the middle.

3 Sprinkle the liqueur over the fruit. Whip the cream until thick and put in a decorator's bag. Pipe a rosette of cream in the middle of the flan.

Serves 6

Gooseberry Tart

¼ lb. butter
1⅔ cups butter cookie crumbs
1 teaspoon cinnamon
1 lb. canned gooseberries
1½ teaspoons unflavored gelatin

1 Use a little butter to grease a fluted flan pan. Melt the rest of the butter and mix it with the cookie crumbs and the cinnamon. Press the mixture evenly around the base and sides of the pan. Chill until set.

2 Drain the canned gooseberries, reserving the syrup. Arrange the gooseberries evenly over the crust.

3 Soften the gelatin in the syrup

Raspberry Rumba, Blueberry Belle and Gooseberry Tart are three simple tarts which are all made with a different base

for 5 minutes, then stand the bowl in a pan of hot water and stir until the gelatin is completely dissolved. Measure the liquid and make up to 1¼ cups with cold water, if necessary. Allow to cool until almost set, then pour over the gooseberries to cover. Chill until set.

Serves 6

Blueberry Belle

dough for one 9-inch pie crust
4 cups blueberries
½ cup sugar
¼ cup water

1034

Festive Fruit Tarts are easy to make — just fill them with your favorite fruits and garnish with almonds and cherries

1 tablespoon cornstarch

1 Preheat the oven to 400°F. Roll out the pie crust to $\frac{1}{4}$ inch thickness on a floured board. Line a flan pan with the dough and prick it with a fork. Trim off excess dough and pinch the rim into a decorative border. Bake for 20-25 minutes; remove from the oven and cool.

2 Meanwhile, wash the blueberries and remove the stalks. Place them in a pan with the sugar and water, cover and cook for 5-10 minutes over gentle heat, stirring from time to time. When the berries are cooked and tender, thicken the juice by stirring in the cornstarch dissolved in a little cold water.

3 Turn the shell out onto a serving dish. Spoon the blueberries into the crust and level them out. Pour in the thickened juice. Serve with whipped cream.

Serves 6

Tip: To enrich the flavor of the flan, add a pinch of cinnamon to the cooked fruit.

Festive Fruit Tarts

dough for one 9-inch pie crust
$\frac{3}{4}$ cup apricot jam
1 tablespoon orange juice
7 mandarin orange sections
10 strawberries
$\frac{3}{4}$ cup sliced almonds
1 green candied cherry
2 apricots
1 tablespoon pistachio nuts
$\frac{1}{2}$ cup red currants
1 banana, sliced

1 Preheat the oven to 400°F. On a floured board, roll the dough out to $\frac{1}{4}$ inch thickness. Lightly butter and flour six tartlet pans and line them with dough. Prick with a fork and bake for 20 minutes. Prepare the apricot glaze: in a saucepan, melt the apricot jam and orange juice and strain.

2 To fill the tarts as shown in the picture, clockwise from top left: arrange 7 mandarin segments in the first. Cover with apricot glaze. In the second, arrange 5 strawberries, interspersed with almonds, and put a green candied cherry in the middle. Glaze lightly.

3 Cut an apricot in half; remove the pit. Put a strawberry in one half and arrange slices of the other half around it. Alternate the slices with pistachio nuts, and glaze. Heap the fourth tart with red currants and stud it with almond slices. Glaze lightly.

4 Cut the rest of the strawberries in half and arrange them in a rosette in the fifth tart. Center with half a strawberry on a slice of banana. Glaze. Fill the sixth tart with banana slices garnished with red currants and pistachio nuts. Glaze. Serve on a dish garnished with the other apricot, halved and filled with red currants.

Serves 6

Banana Cream Flan

dough for one 8-inch pie crust
8-10 sugar lumps
2 large oranges
4-5 ripe bananas
1¼ cups heavy cream

1 Preheat the oven to 400°F.

2 Roll out the dough and use to line an 8-inch flan ring set on a baking sheet. Line with paper, fill with baking beans and bake for 15 minutes. Remove the paper and beans and bake for a further 5 minutes. Remove the flan ring when the flan is cool.

3 Rub the sugar lumps over the orange rind until they are well soaked with the oil. Crush them in a small bowl and add enough orange juice to make a syrup.

4 Slice the bananas, moisten with a little of the orange syrup and spoon into the flan.

5 Whip the cream until it is just thick, and add the remaining orange syrup. Spread the cream thickly over the bananas.

Serves 6

Almond Cheesecake

⅓ cup butter
2 tablespoons lard or shortening
1⅔ cups flour
⅓ cup ground almonds
3 tablespoons sugar
1 egg yolk
1-2 tablespoons water
½ teaspoon vanilla extract

For the Filling:
¼ cup butter
¼ cup sugar
1⅔ cups cottage cheese
2 eggs, beaten

⅓ cup dried currants
finely grated rind ½ orange
2 drops almond extract

1 Preheat the oven to 375°F.

2 Make the pastry: rub the lard or shortening into the flour, add the almonds and sugar and bind with the egg yolk, water and vanilla.

3 Roll out the pastry and use to line an 8-inch flan ring, set on a baking sheet.

4 Prepare the filling: cream together the butter and sugar until light. Strain the cheese and stir into the butter and sugar with the beaten eggs, currants, orange rind and almond extract. Pour into the crust.

5 Bake in the preheated oven for 30 minutes. Cool slightly before removing the flan ring, and serve warm or cold.

Serves 6

Meringue Mincemeat Tart

dough for one 8-inch pie crust
1½ cups mincemeat
1 egg white
¼ cup sugar
candied cherries and angelica

1 Preheat the oven to 400°F.

2 Roll out the dough and use it to line an 8-inch flan ring set on a baking sheet. Bake for 20 minutes. Remove from the oven and reduce the temperature to 375°F.

3 Fill the flan shell with the mincemeat.

4 Beat the egg white until it is softly peaking, add half of the sugar and continue to beat until the mixture is glossy and forms peaks. Gently fold in the remaining sugar and transfer to a decorator's bag fitted with a large star nozzle. Pipe a border of swirls just inside the flan edge and bake in the oven for

15-20 minutes, until set and lightly browned. Decorate with pieces of cherry and angelica.

Serves 6

Mincemeat Party Tarts

dough for one 9-inch pie crust
1½ cups mincemeat

For the Toppings:
¼ cup unsalted butter
¼ cup sugar
1 tablespoon brandy
¼ lb. marzipan

1 Preheat the oven to 375°F.

2 Make the brandy butter: cream the butter thoroughly. Beat in the sugar a little at a time and continue to beat until the mixture is white. Gradually beat in the brandy, then chill until quite firm.

3 Roll out the marzipan about ¼ inch thick and cut 8 or 9 circles with a 2-inch fluted cutter.

4 Roll out the dough thinly and use to line 16-18 tartlet pans. Prick the bases with a fork and bake in the preheated oven for 8 minutes. Put a heaping teaspoonful of mincemeat into each tartlet and bake for a further 6-8 minutes until the mincemeat is hot and the pastry light golden. Cool slightly on a wire rack.

5 Top half of the warm mincemeat pies with a swirl of brandy butter. Cover the other pies with marzipan lids.

Makes 16–18

Meringue Mincemeat Tart (in the background) and Mincemeat Party Tarts taste good at Thanksgiving or at any other time of year

Jam Tart

dough for one 9-inch pie crust
1 tablespoon each of 12 different
  colored jams
2 tablespoons strawberry jam

1 Roll out the dough on a lightly floured board to a thickness of $\frac{1}{4}$ inch and use it to line a 9-inch pie plate. Cut off and reserve the trimmings. Prick the bottom of the crust and leave it to rest for 30 minutes.

2 Preheat the oven to 375°F.

3 With the point of a knife lightly mark the outline of 2 overlapping triangles on the bottom of the dish so that the points of each triangle face in opposite directions to form a six-pointed star.

4 Place a different jam in each of the twelve triangles and spread the strawberry jam in the center.

5 Roll out the pastry trimmings and cut six $\frac{1}{2}$-inch wide strips long enough to cover the tart. Moisten the pastry edges with a little water and arrange the strips over the jam to form the six-pointed star. Bake in the oven for 15 minutes.

Serves 6

Cherry and Almond Tart

2$\frac{1}{4}$ cups flour, sifted
$\frac{1}{4}$ cup butter
$\frac{1}{4}$ cup lard
2 tablespoons water

For the Filling:
1 lb. fresh cherries
1 tablespoon sugar
$\frac{1}{4}$ cup butter
$\frac{1}{4}$ cup sugar
1 large egg, beaten
few drops almond extract
$\frac{1}{3}$ cup ground almonds

2 tablespoons sliced almonds

1 Place the flour in a bowl and rub in the butter and lard until the mixture resembles fine breadcrumbs. Stir the water into the dough and knead it on a floured board until smooth. Chill in the refrigerator for 30 minutes.

2 Preheat the oven to 400°F.

3 Roll out the dough on a lightly floured board to a thickness of $\frac{1}{4}$ inch and use it to line an 8-inch flan pan. Line the inside with wax paper

---

Jam Tart — 12 different flavored jams make it a colorful dessert

and bake the crust for 10 minutes.

4 Remove the crust from the oven and line the base with the cherries. Sprinkle on the sugar.

5 Cream together the butter and sugar until soft and fluffy. Beat in the egg and almond extract and fold in the ground almonds. Spoon on the fruit and sprinkle with the sliced almonds.

6 Reduce the oven heat to 350°F. and bake the tart in the oven for 30-40 minutes until golden. Serve immediately.

Serves 6

Honey Tart

dough for one 9-inch pie crust
⅓ cup corn syrup
1 tablespoon honey
juice and grated rind 1 lemon
2 cups cornflakes

1 Preheat the oven to 425°F. Roll out the dough on a lightly floured board to a thickness of ¼ inch and line a 9-inch pie plate. Trim the edges, reserving the trimmings. Flute the edges or decorate with a fork.

2 In a bowl, blend together the corn syrup, honey, lemon juice and rind.

3 Place the cornflakes in a plastic bag and crush them with a rolling pin. Add the crushed flakes to the bowl and mix them in thoroughly.

4 Prick the pastry with a fork. Spoon the filling into the pie plate and spread it evenly with the back of a spoon.

5 Roll out the remaining dough and cut it into strips. Place the strips on top of the tart in a lattice pattern, sealing the edges as you go.

Honey Tart is sure to be a firm favorite with the children, with its sticky filling and lattice topping

Bake the tart in the oven for 15-20 minutes or until the pastry is golden brown. Serve immediately with hot custard.

Serves 6

Ice Cream Tart

1¼ cups vanilla ice cream
2 eggs, separated
1 whole egg
½ cup honey
pinch salt
2 teaspoons instant coffee granules
¼ cup evaporated milk
2 teaspoons rum
⅔ cup heavy cream, whipped
2 tablespoons sliced almonds

1 Spread the ice cream ¼ inch thick over the base and sides of a 9-inch freezerproof pie dish. Immediately place it in the freezer.

2 In a bowl beat together the egg yolks and whole egg. Gradually stir in half of the honey, the salt, coffee granules and evaporated milk.

3 Place the bowl over a saucepan of simmering water and cook the egg and honey mixture, stirring frequently, for 10 minutes or until it is thick and creamy. Remove the bowl from the heat, stir in the rum and let the mixture cool.

4 Beat the egg whites until they are stiff and beat in the remaining honey, adding it in a thin trickle.

5 Fold the egg white mixture into the egg and honey mixture. Fold in the whipped cream. When ready to serve, remove the ice cream ''crust'' from the freezer and spread the inside with the mixture. Sprinkle the almonds over the top and serve.

Serves 6

Look 'n Cook Apple Bakewell Tart

1 The ingredients: pie crust dough, apples, flour, sugar, ground almonds, eggs, butter, coffee liqueur **2** Roll out cook the dough to line a buttered 8-inch flan pan **3** Prick the base of the crust with a fork **4** Peel and core the apples and slice them in rings. Sauté them gently in butter and honey until tender **5** Place the apple slices in the flan shell **6** Beat the butter and sugar. Add the beaten eggs, liqueur, flour and ground almonds to

make a thick paste **7** With a spatula, spread the paste evenly over the layer of apple rings **8** Cut the dough trimmings into narrow strips. Place these in a lattice pattern across the flan **9** Brush the lattice strips with beaten egg. Dust the flan with confectioners' sugar and bake in a moderate oven for 30-40 minutes **10** Cool and serve with custard or cream

Apple Bakewell Tart

dough for one 8-inch pie crust
2 apples
1 tablespoon butter
1 tablespoon honey
¼ lb. butter
½ cup sugar
2 eggs, beaten
2 tablespoons coffee-flavored liqueur
½ cup flour
¾ cup ground almonds
1 tablespoon confectioners' sugar

1 On a floured board, roll out the dough to ¼ inch thick, and line a buttered 8-inch fluted flan pan. Prick the base of the flan with a fork.

2 Peel and core the apples and cut them in rings. Cook them in a skillet with 1 tablespoon butter and honey for 5-10 minutes until tender. Place the apple slices in the base of the crust.

3 Preheat the oven to 375°F.

4 In a mixing bowl, cream together the remaining butter and sugar until fluffy. Reserve 2 teaspoons of the beaten egg and mix the rest of the egg into the butter and sugar. Add the liqueur.

5 Fold in the flour and the ground almonds and mix to a thick, smooth paste. Spread the paste evenly over the layer of apples in the flan.

6 Cut the dough trimmings into strips ½ inch wide and place these in a lattice pattern across the flan. Brush the lattice strips with the reserved beaten egg and sprinkle the flan with the confectioners' sugar. Bake for 30-40 minutes, allow to cool and serve with cream.

Serves 6–8

Tip: The traditional Bakewell Tart does not include fruit, but a layer of jam. The tart may also be iced with a thin layer of white icing instead of the lattice pattern.

You can also add 2 tablespoons of currants to the almond paste.

Mandarin Crisp

1 cup gingersnap cookie crumbs
2 tablespoons butter
2 ozs. bitter chocolate
¼ cup orange-flavored gelatin
⅔ cup hot water
⅔ cup evaporated milk
grated rind ½ orange
4 ozs. canned mandarin orange sections

1 Place the cookie crumbs in a bowl. Melt the butter and chocolate together and mix them into the crumbs. Lightly grease a 9-inch flan pan and spoon the crumb mixture into it, pressing it evenly and tightly around the sides and base. Chill in the refrigerator until set.

2 Melt the gelatin in a pan with the water. In a bowl, beat the evaporated milk until thick. Fold in the grated orange rind and the melted gelatin.

3 When the mixture is nearly set, pour it into the crumb shell. Drain the mandarin segments and arrange them over the top. Chill until set. Serve garnished with whipped cream.

Serves 6–8

Foolish Tart

1 lb. rhubarb
½ cup sugar
2 tablespoons water
pinch ground ginger
½ teaspoon cinnamon
one 10-inch sponge cake shell
⅓ cup apricot jam
⅔ cup heavy cream

1 Wash the rhubarb thoroughly and cut it into 1¼-inch lengths. Put the rhubarb, sugar, water, ginger and cinnamon in a pan, cover and cook over low heat until the fruit is soft and pulpy. Strain off any excess water and mash the fruit pulp to a purée.

2 Place the sponge shell on a serving dish. Spread the base and sides with apricot jam.

3 Beat the cream until stiff. Fold in the rhubarb purée and pour the mixture into the shell. Chill in the refrigerator until the filling is set, and serve.

Serves 6–8

Pineapple Flan

dough for one 9-inch pie crust
8 canned pineapple rings
1¼ cups pastry cream or very thick custard
7 strawberries

1 Preheat the oven to 375°F.

2 Roll out the pie crust on a floured board, and line a 9-inch flan pan.

3 Finely chop one of the pineapple rings, and mix it into the pastry cream. Pour into the crust. Bake for 30-40 minutes until just golden brown. Remove from the pan and allow to cool.

4 Drain the rest of the canned pineapple rings and arrange them in an overlapping circle around the flan. Place a strawberry in the middle of each pineapple ring. Serve with cream or custard.

Serves 6

Pineapple Flan is a golden delight with different textures — crisp pastry, a creamy filling and fresh juicy pineapple

1 Put the currants in a bowl of boiling water and leave them to stand for 10 minutes. Drain and let them cool.

2 Roll out the dough on a floured board. Using a 2½-inch fluted cutter, stamp out 12 rounds and use them to line twelve 2½-inch tartlet tins.

3 Melt the butter in a small pan. Remove it from the heat and stir in the sugar, cream, rum, and egg yolk.

4 Using a teaspoon, divide the mixture evenly between the small tarts. Do not let the filling come more than ¾ up the sides of the dough. Bake in the oven for 15-20 minutes or until the dough is crisp and the filling golden.

Makes 12

Coconut Tartlets

dough for one 9-inch pie crust
¼ cup butter
¼ cup sugar
1 egg, beaten
⅔ cup shredded coconut
3 tablespoons self-rising flour
2 tablespoons raspberry jam

1 Roll out the dough on a floured board, and, using a 2½-inch cutter, cut 12 rounds. Use them to line 12 tartlet tins.

2 Preheat the oven to 375°F. Cream the butter and sugar and beat in the egg. Fold in the coconut and flour with a metal spoon.

3 Place a little jam and then a spoonful of the coconut mixture into each pastry shell. Bake in the oven for 15 minutes, until golden and firm to the touch.

Makes 12 tartlets

Sugar Plum Flan has an unusual filling of plums in a cinnamon and yogurt flavored custard studded with almonds

Sugar Plum Flan

1⅔ cups flour
¼ teaspoon salt
6 tablespoons butter
2 teaspoons sugar
1 tablespoon milk
4 egg yolks
1 tablespoon sugar
⅔ cup yogurt
½ teaspoon cinnamon
1 lb. Italian damson plums
⅓ cup blanched almonds
3 tablespoons brown sugar

1 Preheat the oven to 400°F.

2 Sift the flour and salt into a bowl. Rub in the butter until it re-sembles fine breadcrumbs. Stir in the sugar and bind the mixture together with the milk and one of the 4 egg yolks.

3 Roll out the dough to line an 8-inch flan ring. Place the remaining 3 egg yolks, the sugar, yogurt and cinnamon in a bowl and blend them thoroughly. Pour this mixture into the pastry shell.

4 Cut the plums in half and remove their pits. Arrange them over the top of the flan, cut side up. Place the flan in the oven for 35-40 minutes.

5 Preheat the broiler. Remove the flan from the oven and place a blanched almond in the center of each plum. Sprinkle with the brown sugar and place it under the broiler until the top is golden.

Serves 6

1043

Apricot Cream Tartlets

dough for one 9-inch pie crust
1 egg white
¼ cup sugar
1¼ cups pastry cream or very thick custard
⅓ cup apricot jam

Apricot Cream Tartlets are very light and simple— a creamy filling topped with swirls of fluffy meringue

1 Preheat the oven to 375°F. Roll out the pie crust to line 6 small tartlet tins. Bake for 8-10 minutes, then remove from the oven.

2 Meanwhile, beat the egg white until stiff. Gradually fold in the sugar. Place the mixture in a decorator's bag.

3 Fill the base of the tartlets with pastry cream. Spread apricot jam on top of each one. Pipe rosettes of meringue around the edge of each tart. Return to the oven for 5 minutes until the meringue is lightly toasted. Cool and serve.

Serves 6

Yellow Plum Tart

dough for one 10-inch pie crust
1 lb. yellow plums
⅔ cup sweet white wine
⅔ cup water
1⅓ cups sugar
5 egg yolks
1 cup + 2 tablespoons flour
1⅞ cups milk
½ teaspoon vanilla extract

1 Preheat the oven to 400°F. Roll out the dough to line a 10-inch flan pan and bake for 15-20 minutes. Remove from the oven and cool.

2 Meanwhile, place the plums, white wine, water, and ¼ cup of the sugar in a pan. Simmer gently over low heat for about 5 minutes until the plums are tender. Cool in the syrup.

3 In a mixing bowl, beat the egg yolks, then gradually add the flour and the rest of the sugar. Pour in the milk, beating all the time to produce a smooth mixture. Add the vanilla and a little of the plum syrup. Place in a pan and heat gently, stirring, until the mixture thickens.

4 Pour the thickened custard into the crust. With a slotted spoon,

Tarte Basque

¼ cup butter, softened
3 cups flour
4 egg yolks
pinch salt
2 teaspoons baking powder
½ cup sugar
½ cup milk

For the Filling:
6 large cooking apples
juice 1 lemon
5 tablespoons butter
⅔ cup sugar
1 tablespoon cinnamon
2 tablespoons brown sugar

1 Cut the butter into small pieces.

2 Sift the flour into a bowl. Beat in the egg yolks, salt, baking powder, sugar and butter pieces until you have a smooth firm dough.

3 Preheat the oven to 400°F.

4 Roll out the dough on a floured board to a thickness of ¼ inch. Cut a ring of the dough to line a well-greased and -floured 8-inch tart pan. Prick the pastry and bake in the oven for 20-25 minutes.

5 Peel, core and thickly slice the apples and sprinkle them with the lemon juice to prevent them from discoloring.

6 Melt ¾ of the butter in a skillet. Add the apple slices; sprinkle them with the sugar and cinnamon. Gently sauté them on both sides until they are golden.

7 Remove the crust from the oven and fill it with 2 layers of overlapping apple slices.

Tarte Basque is bound to be popular — overflowing with glazed, soft apple slices flavored with cinnamon

8 Sprinkle the apples with the brown sugar and place a few pats of the remaining butter on top. Return the tart to the oven for 5 minutes and serve immediately.

Serves 6

Rum and Butter Tartlets

½ cup dried currants
dough for one 9-inch pie crust
2 tablespoons butter
½ cup soft brown sugar
1 tablespoon light cream
2 tablespoons rum
1 egg yolk, beaten

drain the plums and arrange them on top of the custard mixture. Chill and serve cold.

Serves 6–8

Rice Tart

¼ cup butter
¼ cup lard or shortening
2¼ cups flour
1 tablespoon brandy, sherry or rum
1 tablespoon light cream or sour cream
1 tablespoon water
⅓ cup sugar
pinch salt

For the Filling:
⅔ cup short-grain rice
3 cups milk

2 eggs, separated
pinch salt
¼ cup sugar
½ teaspoon cinnamon
1½ tablespoons finely chopped almonds

1 Rub the butter and lard or shortening into the flour in a mixing bowl. Make a well in the middle and pour in the liquor, cream or sour cream, water, sugar and salt. Blend and knead lightly to a dough. Leave in a cool place for 1 hour.

2 Meanwhile, rinse the rice for the filling and cook it in a pan of boiling water for 3 minutes. Drain and rinse in cold water.

3 Place the milk in a pan and bring it to a boil. Add the rice and cook

---

Yellow Plum Tart is bubbling with sunny golden plums set in a smooth, creamy base of pastry cream

over very low heat for about 10 minutes. Stir in the egg yolks, salt, sugar, cinnamon and chopped almonds.

4 In a bowl beat the egg whites until stiff. Fold them into the rice mixture.

5 Preheat the oven to 350°F. On a floured board roll out the pie crust dough and use it to line a 9-inch lightly greased flan pan. Pour the rice mixture into the crust. Bake in the oven for about 45 minutes. Serve hot or cold.

Serves 6

Tip: This flan goes well with fresh or canned fruit, such as plums or mandarin oranges. To make an Apple and Rice Flan, halve the quantities for the filling and cover the base of the crust with slices of peeled, cored cooking apples sprinkled with sugar, then top with the rice.

Chocolate Meringue Flan

dough for one 8-inch pie crust
3 tablespoons cornstarch
¼ cup cocoa
⅔ cup sugar
1¾ cups milk
¼ cup butter
3 egg yolks
½ teaspoon vanilla extract

For the Meringue:
3 egg whites
⅓ cup sugar

1 Preheat the oven to 400°F. Prepare an 8-inch flan crust and bake it. Let it cool.

2 In a mixing bowl, blend together the cornstarch, cocoa and sugar. Warm the milk and add it gradually to this mixture. Return it to the pan and cook, stirring, over gentle heat until the mixture thickens.

3 Remove the pan from the heat. Stir in the butter and egg yolks and flavor with a little vanilla. Pour the mixture into the crust.

4 In another bowl beat the egg whites until stiff. Gradually add the sugar. Spoon the meringue over the chocolate filling. Bake for about 15 minutes until the meringue is crisp and golden on top. Cool before serving.

Serves 6

Amandine Tarts, crunchy with almonds and garnished with cherries, can be served either at dinner or at a tea party

Amandine Tarts

dough for one 9-inch pie crust
¼ cup butter
¼ cup sugar
1 egg, beaten
⅓ cup ground almonds
2 tablespoons flour
few drops almond extract
⅓ cup sliced almonds
¼ cup apricot jam
6 candied cherries

1 Preheat the oven to 375°F.

2 On a floured board roll out the dough to ¼ inch thick and line 6 greased and floured tart tins. Bake for 20 minutes, then remove from the oven, leaving the oven on.

3 Meanwhile, cream the butter with the sugar until pale and fluffy. Gradually add the egg. Then beat in

the ground almonds, sifted flour, and flavor with a little almond extract.

4 Fill the half-cooked tart shells with the almond paste. Cover with sliced almonds and return to the oven for 10 minutes or until the dough is cooked.

5 Melt the apricot jam in a pan over low heat, adding a little water if necessary. Top each tart with a cherry and spread with apricot glaze. Cool before serving.

Serves 6

Cherry Meringue Flan

dough for one 10-inch pie crust
1¼ cups pastry cream or very thick custard
2 teaspoons cherry-flavored liqueur

Cherry Meringue Flan is a real party special, with rings of big luscious cherries set in snowy meringue peaks

1 egg white
¼ cup sugar
½ teaspoon vanilla extract
1 lb. canned tart cherries

1 Preheat the oven to 400°F. Roll out the pie crust to ¼ inch thickness and line a buttered 10-inch flan dish. Prick the dough and bake for 20 minutes.

2 Meanwhile, flavor the pastry cream with the liqueur. Spread it over the base of the cooled crust.

3 Beat the egg white until stiff and fold in the sugar. Flavor with vanilla. Put in a decorator's bag and pipe around the flan and in the middle. Arrange the cherries in a double ring on the flan.

4 Return the flan to the oven for 5 minutes so that the meringue is just

tinged with gold. Let it cool before serving.

Serves 6–8

Edinburgh Tart

dough for one 8-inch pie crust
¼ cup butter, melted
¼ cup sugar
½ cup chopped candied peel
1 tablespoon raisins
½ cup flour
2 eggs, beaten

1 Preheat the oven to 375°F. Roll out the dough to line an 8-inch flan pan.

2 Mix the butter, sugar, peel, raisins and flour. Stir in the eggs and pour into the pastry shell. Bake for 40 minutes, cool and serve.

Serves 6

Pies

Pies are easy to make and can be filled with a variety of fruity fillings. You can use common fruits such as apples, pears and plums, or more exotic tropical fruits such as mangoes and pineapple. Serve a fruit pie with freshly made hot custard or some whipped cream. Pies can be made with either puff or pie crust pastry. For extra special results, try adding some ground almonds or cinnamon to the pie crust mix. The flavor of apple and pear pies is more interesting if you add a pinch of cinnamon and some cloves and serve with Cheddar cheese.

Deep Dish Spicy Apple Pie

4-5 cooking apples
butter
½ teaspoon cinnamon
½ cup brown sugar
4 cloves
grated rind and juice 1 lemon
3 tablespoons water
dough for one 9-inch pie crust
2 teaspoons milk
2 tablespoons sugar

1 Peel, core and thinly slice the apples. Butter a deep pie dish and arrange the apples inside in layers with the cinnamon and brown sugar. Spike some apple slices with the cloves and sprinkle the grated lemon rind and juice over the top. Add the water.

2 Preheat the oven to 400°F. Roll out the dough to the diameter of the pie dish and use to cover the pie. Trim around the edge and seal firmly. Crimp and decorate it if you wish. Make a small incision in the top of the pie with a sharp knife.

3 Brush with milk and sprinkle with sugar. Bake in the oven and reduce the temperature to 350°F. after 10 minutes. Bake for another 20 minutes until the pie is cooked and golden brown. Serve hot or cold, with cream.

Serves 6

Deep Dish Pumpkin Pie

½ lb. pumpkin, peeled and seeded
½ lb. cooking apples, peeled and cored
⅔ cup dried currants
¼ cup chopped mixed peel
1 teaspoon mixed ground clove and cinnamon
butter
¼ cup soft brown sugar
1 tablespoon water
dough for one 9-inch pie crust
1 teaspoon milk
2 tablespoons sugar

1 Cut the pumpkin and apples into cubes and mix with the currants, mixed peel and spice.

2 Butter a deep pie dish and fill with the fruit mixture. Sprinkle on the soft brown sugar and add the water.

3 Preheat the oven to 400°F. Roll out the dough to a large circle, the same diameter as the pie dish. Wet the rim of the dish and cover with the dough. Trim and crimp the edges and make a small hole in the top. Brush with milk and sprinkle with sugar.

4 Bake in the oven for 10 minutes, then reduce the temperature to 350°F. and bake for a further 30 minutes until crisp and golden brown. Serve with whipped cream.

Serves 6

Spiced Date and Pear Pie

¼ lb. butter
1 cup whole wheat flour
½ cup rolled oats
water to mix
butter for greasing
½ cup dates, seeded and chopped
4 dessert pears, peeled, cored and sliced
½ teaspoon cinnamon
grated rind and juice ½ lemon
¼ cup soft brown sugar
1 teaspoon milk
2 tablespoons sugar

1 Rub the butter into the flour and oats with your fingertips. Then mix in enough water to make a stiff pastry dough. Roll out half of the dough on a floured surface and use it to line a 7-inch greased shallow pie dish.

2 Preheat the oven to 425°F.

3 Place the dates, pears, cinnamon, lemon rind, juice and brown sugar inside the pie. Roll out the remaining dough to make a lid. Cover the pie, then trim and crimp the edges. Brush the lid of the pie with milk and sprinkle on the sugar.

4 Bake in the oven for 10 minutes, then reduce the temperature to 375°F. for the remaining 20 minutes. Remove the pie when it is crisp and golden brown. Serve the pie hot with whipped cream or hot custard.

Serves 6

Tips: If fresh pears are not available, you can make this pie using the same weight of drained canned pears. Also, if you prefer plain pastry, you can make it with ordinary white flour instead of whole wheat flour.

Spicy Apple Pie is one of the world's classic desserts; it is excellent to follow a good hearty dinner of roast meat

Rhubarb Pie

dough for two 9-inch pie crusts
10 sticks rhubarb cut into ½-inch
  pieces
1½ cups sugar
2 tablespoons butter
grated rind 1 orange
2 tablespoons cornstarch
¼ cup orange juice
½ teaspoon cinnamon
1 egg yolk
2 tablespoons milk
¼ cup confectioners' sugar

1 Preheat the oven to 400°F. Roll out the dough on a floured board to a thickness of ¼ inch. Use half to line the bottom and sides of a 9-inch pie plate.

2 Arrange the rhubarb over the bottom of the dish. Add the sugar, butter and orange rind.

3 Blend the cornstarch with the orange juice and pour it over the other ingredients. Sprinkle with the cinnamon and cover with the second round of dough. Brush the top with the egg yolk mixed with milk and bake the pie in the oven for 30 minutes or until the crust is golden.

4 Dust with the confectioners' sugar and serve.

Serves 6

Rum and Date Pie

3⅓ cups flour
1¼ cups butter
¼ cup sugar
1 egg yolk
2 tablespoons cold water
butter
½ cup chopped dates
¼ cup chopped preserved ginger
2 tablespoons rum

1 Preheat the oven to 400°F. Sift

the flour into a bowl. Cut 1 cup of the butter into pieces and rub it into the flour until the mixture resembles fine breadcrumbs. Stir in 2 teaspoons of the sugar. Blend the egg yolk and water together and pour into the flour, mixing quickly to form a firm dough. Turn the dough onto a floured board and knead lightly until it is smooth. Roll out the dough to a thickness of ¼ inch.

2 Line a well-buttered pie plate with half the dough and cover it with the dates and ginger.

3 Cream together the remaining butter and sugar and the rum and spread it over the filling.

4 Cover with the remaining dough and bake the pie in the preheated oven for 15 minutes. Reduce the heat to 350°F. and bake for a further 30 minutes.

Serves 6

Orange Raisin Pie

dough for two 8-inch pie crusts
2 cups raisins
2 tablespoons orange juice
2 tablespoons corn syrup
2 tablespoons confectioners' sugar

1 Preheat the oven to 425°F.

2 Roll out the dough on a lightly floured board to a thickness of ¼ inch. Use half to line an 8-inch pie plate. Trim the edges.

3 In a bowl blend together the raisins, orange juice and syrup. Spread the mixture evenly over the pie plate. Sprinkle the rims of the plate with a little water and arrange the remaining dough, being careful not to stretch it, over the top. Seal the rims with your fingers and cut off any trimmings.

4 Bake the pie on the middle shelf

of the oven for 25-30 minutes. Sprinkle with the confectioner's sugar and serve.

Serves 6

Apple and Blackberry Pie

2-3 cooking apples
1½ cups blackberries
dough for two 9-inch pie crusts
butter for greasing
⅓ cup sugar
1 tablespoon water
beaten egg for glazing

1 Peel, core, quarter and cut the apples into slices. Remove the stalks from the blackberries and wash them thoroughly.

2 Preheat the oven to 400°F.

3 Roll out the dough on a floured board to a thickness of ¼ inch. Use half the dough to line a buttered 3¾-cup pie dish. Cut off and reserve the trimmings. Cover the base with half the apples and blackberries. Add the sugar and water and then the remaining fruit.

4 Dampen the rim of the pie plate and cover the pie with the remaining dough. Seal and flute the edges. Decorate the top with 5 leaves made from the reserved pastry trimmings and brush it with the beaten egg. Place the dish on a baking sheet and bake it for 10 minutes in the preheated oven. Reduce the heat to 350°F. and cook for a further 30 minutes. If the dough browns too quickly, cover it with foil. Serve hot.

Serves 6–8

Apple and Blackberry Pie is full of natural country goodness. For added flavor, try sprinkling in grated lemon or cinnamon

Greengage Pie

1⅔ cups flour
pinch salt
3 tablespoons butter
3 tablespoons lard or shortening
2 tablespoons water

For the Filling:
1½ lbs. greengage plums
½ cup sugar
2 tablespoons water
1 teaspoon cinnamon

1 Sift the flour and salt into a bowl. Rub in the butter and lard or shortening until the mixture resembles fine crumbs. Gradually add the water, stirring with a spatula, until the dough starts to stick together. Knead lightly and set aside for 15 minutes.

2 Wash the fruit and remove any pieces of stalk. Arrange them in a large pie dish and sprinkle with the sugar, water and cinnamon.

3 Preheat the oven to 425°F. Roll out the dough to ¼ inch thick, about 1 inch larger in diameter than the pie dish. Cut a strip the width of the dish rim, dampen the rim and stick the strip around. Dampen the strip and lay the rest of the dough across the pie. Cut off any excess and crimp the edges with a fork. Use leftover dough to make leaves to decorate the top.

4 Bake for 15 minutes, then lower the oven heat to 350°F. Bake for 20-30 minutes until the fruit is cooked. Serve hot or cold, with whipped cream.

Serves 6

Greengage Pie would be ideal for Sunday lunch, with its light pastry shell and filling of tender, juicy, hot plums

Exotic Pie

3⅓ cups flour
pinch salt
⅓ cup butter
⅓ cup lard or shortening
1 tablespoon sugar
¼ cup water

For the Filling:
1 cup strawberries
½ lb. litchis
2-lb. pineapple
3 bananas
2 mangoes
juice ½ lemon
¼ cup rum
2 tablespoons brown sugar

1 Sift the flour into a mixing bowl with the salt. Rub in the butter and the lard or shortening to make fine crumbs. Add the sugar. Stir with a knife while adding the water, little by little, until the mixture begins to stick together. Knead lightly to form a smooth dough. Leave it to rest for 15 minutes.

2 Prepare the fruit: wash and hull the strawberries. If using fresh litchis, peel them. Peel the pineapple and remove the dark spots, and cut into cubes. Peel and slice the bananas. Cut the mango flesh into chunks.

3 Preheat the oven to 400°F. Roll out the dough on a floured board to cover a large 9 cup pie dish. Mix the fruits and arrange them in the dish. Sprinkle with the lemon juice, rum and brown sugar. Place the dough over the top, cut off any excess around the sides and crimp the edges. With the point of a sharp knife, cut out a star shape from the middle of the dough. Bake in the oven for 20-25 minutes; serve hot or cold.

Serves 8

Tip: Before serving, pour thick cream through the star-shaped hole into the pie underneath.

Exotic Pie owes its name to the filling of unusual fruits—litchis, pineapple, mango and banana

Raspberry Pie

5 cups raspberries
butter
1 tablespoon cornstarch
¼ cup sugar
pinch nutmeg
few drops almond extract
dough for one 9-inch pie crust
1 teaspoon milk
sugar for dusting

1 Preheat the oven to 400°F. Wash, drain and hull the raspberries. Place them in a deep buttered pie dish and sprinkle the cornstarch between the layers — this will thicken the syrup. Add the sugar, nutmeg and almond extract.

2 Roll out the dough on a floured surface to the diameter of the pie dish. Dampen the edges of the pie dish and cover the top with the dough. Trim and crimp the edges and make a small hole in the top with a sharp knife. Brush with milk.

3 Bake in the oven and, after 10 minutes, reduce the temperature to 350°F. Cook for a further 20 minutes until crisp and golden. Just before serving, dust generously with sugar.

Serves 6

Crusty Plum Pie

butter
1½ lbs. Italian damson plums
½ cup sugar
½ teaspoon cinnamon
1 tablespoon water
dough for one 9-inch pie crust
1 teaspoon milk
sugar for dusting

1 Butter a deep pie dish and preheat the oven to 400°F.

2 Fill the pie dish with the plums, sugar, cinnamon and water.

3 Roll out the pie crust to the diameter of the pie dish. Cover the pie with the dough lid. Trim and crimp the edges, then brush lightly with the milk and dust with sugar.

4 Place in the oven and, after 10 minutes, reduce the temperature to 350°F. Bake for another 20 minutes until crisp and golden. Serve with cream or custard.

Serves 6

Tip: You can always use greengage plums in this pie for an unusual variation — cook them in exactly the same way.

Raspberry Pie is just right for feeding the family — whatever the weather — serve it cold with cream or hot with custard

Customer service: Box 1000, Brattleboro, VT 05301

Text typesetting in Times Roman and Souvenir
by A & B Typesetters, Inc., Concord   NH
Indexes in Helvetica by WordTech Corpor-
ation, Woburn   MA
Covers by Federated Lithographers,
Providence   RI
Printing and binding by Rand McNally,
Versailles   KY
Design and production by Unicorn Produc-
tion Services, Boston   MA
Publisher   Tom Begner
Editorial production: Kathy Shulga, Michael
Michaud
Staff: Erika Petersson, Pam Thompson

© Illustrations Bay Books Pty Ltd., Sydney,
Australia. Reprinted by permission.
© Illustrations from
"Les Cours de la Cuisine A à Z"
"Femmes d'Aujourd'hui"

ISBN 0-914575-11-2

For easy reference, the volumes are numbered
as follows.

1	1-96
2	97-192
3	193-288
4	289-384
5	385-480
6	481-576
7	577-672
8	673-768
9	769-864
10	865-960
11	961-1056
12	1057-1152